1 Angel Square

Square

Len Grant

MANCHESTER
1824

Manchester University Press

Colophon

Published by Manchester University Press
Oxford Road, Manchester M13 9NR, UK
and Room 400, 175 Fifth Avenue, New York, NY 10010, USA
www.manchesteruniversitypress.co.uk

Distributed in the United States exclusively by
Palgrave Macmillan, 175 Fifth Avenue, New York,
NY 10010, USA

Distributed in Canada exclusively by
UBC Press, University of British Columbia, 2029 West Mall, Vancouver, BC,
Canada V6T 1Z2

British Library Cataloguing-in-Publication Data
A catalogue record for this book is available from the British Library

Library of Congress Cataloging-in-Publication Data applied for

First published 2013

ISBN: 978 0 7190 9110 0

All images by Len Grant except pp. 10 and 29, National Co-operative Archive;
pp. 13, 20-25, Courtesy of Manchester Libraries, Information and Archives,
Manchester City Council;
p. 25, Oxford Archaeology North; pp. 27, 30-35, 71, 74, 3DReid;
p. 36, BAM Construct UK Ltd; p. 37, Karen Wright Photography;
p. 118, The Co-operative Group;
pp. 38 and 39, Fagan Jones Communications Ltd; p. 115 (top), Scape.

© Len Grant 2013 (www.lengrant.co.uk)
Design: Alan Ward (www.axisgraphicdesign.co.uk)
Print: DeckersSnoeck, Antwerp, Belgium

To find out more about 1 Angel Square and the wider NOMA development
visit: www.noma53.com

Contents

Foreword

1 Angel Square is a stunning example of what can be achieved when a business such as The Co-operative Group marries its values and principles with a commercially sound approach to architecture and construction.

But much more than this, The Co-operative has created an iconic, 21st century building that happily stands shoulder to shoulder with the other landmark properties that have been part of the Group's legacy in Manchester since the 1900s.

It is also a shining example of how creating a new property can bring prosperity to the entire region: apprenticeships made up 7.6% of workers on site, 54% of the workforce were from Greater Manchester, and 108 contracts were awarded to Greater Manchester contractors.

As Chief Executive of Manchester City Council it gives me enormous pride to see such a ground-breaking building located in the heart of the city. Boasting leading edge technology, the environmental credentials of 1 Angel Square are unmatched anywhere else in Europe and, in the future, I would like to see all new properties aspire to its specifications.

With its focus firmly on sustainability and innovation, 1 Angel Square is an example for all architects and constructors to follow, not only in Manchester, but throughout the world.

Sir Howard Bernstein
Chief Executive, Manchester City Council

Welcome Addition

For many passers-by this unusual-looking building on the northern edge of their city centre is something to briefly appraise, maybe even admire, before moving on. For them it's just another addition to the ever-changing urban landscape of this post-industrial city. Mancunians are used to change.

But as these pages reveal, there is more to 1 Angel Square. Far from being just another building, it is currently the UK's greenest office building, having attained the highest ever BREEAM score, an industry standard for measuring environmental sustainability. This on top of a growing tally of construction and design awards.

The fact that the building is here, on this site, is a tale in itself. Although it has been based in Manchester for 150 years, The Co-operative Group originally considered relocating its head office functions outside the city and only a hard-nosed commercial evaluation convinced it to stay. Would it be cheaper to build a new home for 3,000 employees elsewhere in Greater Manchester? Maybe there was more to that decision than property prices and the cost of construction.

Although enjoying the kudos of their heritage buildings, the Group's Manchester employees had long endured outdated, inefficient office environments. Consecutive chief executives had previously side-stepped the impending issue and so by the time Peter Marks headed the Group in 2007, doing nothing about the crumbling estate was no longer an option. Together with retail acquisitions, corporate re-branding and bringing The Co-operative Banking Group into the fold, it became a priority of his tenure.

The site itself can tell another story. Two hundred years ago it was a no-go area, a slum so depraved that even the most seasoned social commentators found its living conditions shocking. Dank cellar dwellings and overcrowded lodging houses were home to the less fortunate inhabitants of what was then a burgeoning cotton town.

Even then Miller Street was at the centre of innovation. The street name is derived from Arkwright's Mill, a five-storey prototype developed by Richard Arkwright and the forerunner to the modern factory system. Perhaps, in its time, that mill was another addition to the urban landscape that passers-by considered, maybe admired, before moving on, unaware of its significance.

The story of this building's design is a fascinating one. As well as being shaped by the environmental aspirations of the client and the constraints of the site, the completed building had to send the right message to The Co-operative Group's stakeholders. It had to be innovative, forward-looking and dynamic. It had to exude confidence and stability, but it had to do all these things subtly, without showing off. This is, after all, a commercial business whose 'shareholders' are more than likely passengers on that cross-town bus or commuters on the incoming tram.

Well into the design process, the architects 3DReid were convinced they had come up with the right solution only to be thrown into a creative turmoil when the client challenged them to make their design more adaptable to a future commercial marketplace. They rose to that challenge, produced a different solution and, in retrospect, acknowledge that they've made a better building.

For the whole project team – architects, engineers, project managers and builders – the creation of 1 Angel Square has been a once-in-a-lifetime opportunity to work together on a career-defining project. It is to their credit that each challenge has been tackled robustly with professionalism and candour. This building will be the focal point of their portfolios, and a piece of the city they can point at and proudly say, "We made that."

The construction process was an exercise in project co-ordination with teams of specialists working shoulder to shoulder to a timetable that allowed little room for unforeseen challenges. But even with such a tight schedule, the BAM Construction team and The Co-operative Group used the construction site as an opportunity to employ and educate. The building's environmental credentials – for example, the use of the Group's homegrown rapeseed oil as a biofuel and the benefits of a 'double skin' façade – are now known to hundreds of primary schoolchildren and university undergraduates.

1 Angel Square is the first new building of the NOMA estate, an £80m mixed-use development that will see this edge of the city move northwards, creating new spaces and new opportunities. It seems right that it is The Co-operative Group that is driving this progress. The retail co-operative movement has been the custodian of this part of our city for a century and a half. It has looked after it well, and made lasting positive contributions, periodically adding architectural icons to the cityscape. 1 Angel Square continues that tradition. It sits well in our city and we are pleased to welcome it.

Len Grant, 2013

Project Granary

As the biofuel heat and power plant fires up and the first of 3,000 head office staff take their seats in front of their 'virtual desktops', it will mark not only the completion of a single building, and the beginnings of a new area for the city, but will be yet another marker in the transformation of perhaps the UK's most iconic retail and financial services business.

The creation of this showpiece of sustainable design and the revival of the retail co-operative business are so intertwined that the story of one cannot be fully appreciated without an understanding of the other.

The consumer co-operative movement goes back to 1844, when rapidly industrialising northern towns were grappling with the social consequences of being at the forefront of the world's economy. Low wages, dreadful housing and inescapable poverty led to living conditions that shocked the most seasoned social commentators, but which the municipal authorities were slow to improve.

Friedrich Engels, in compiling first-hand evidence for his acclaimed book The Condition of the Working Class in England, walked the dead-end passages and ginnels of Manchester's Angel Meadow, no doubt on the exact spot now occupied by 1 Angel Square, and wrote: 'The potatoes which the workers buy are usually poor quality, the vegetables wilted, the cheese old, the bacon rancid, the meat lean, tough, taken from old, often diseased cattle... the sellers are usually small hucksters who buy up inferior goods, and can sell them cheaply by reason of their badness.'

The Co-operative: a business model based on democratically-agreed values and principles.

Self-help

Against this backdrop of unsanitary conditions and third-rate food, a group of weavers – with a clogger, shoemaker, joiner and cabinet maker – in Rochdale decided to band together, buy in bulk and offer discounted, wholesome food to friends, family and co-workers. Their aspiration was originally thwarted, however, as local suppliers refused to sell them any produce. And so, taking turns to push a wooden cart, a handful of founding members made the 24-mile round trip to Manchester, where they purchased butter, sugar, flour and oatmeal to sell in their Toad Lane shop.

The Rochdale Pioneers, as they became known, founded the first consumer co-operative to operate within democratically agreed principles, a business model that was quickly duplicated by socially concerned businessmen throughout the country. Within 10 years there were a thousand co-operatives across Britain.

By 1863, the forerunner to the Co-operative Wholesale Society (CWS) had been created in Manchester by a group of smaller societies looking for ever-greater economies of scale. Primarily a buying and manufacturing group, it was founded by co-operatives rather than individual consumers.

For decades the co-operative model thrived. Every high street had its local branch, every town centre had its distinctive ornate Co-operative building, a confident architectural statement that intentionally offered the society's working class members the same quality of design that might be enjoyed by the wealthy mill owners. As well as butter, sugar and flour, these stores were now offering tea, tobacco, milk, shoes. Much later some of the larger regional societies even sold cars, holidays and funerals. Local shoppers effectively became part owners, their names recorded in huge registers and their patronage rewarded with the 'divi'.

Fast forward to the late 1970s when the local co-operatives began to feel isolated in a rapidly changing retail environment. Tesco was expanding from its south-eastern stronghold acquiring smaller groups of regional supermarkets. Family-owned Sainsbury's was maintained its position as market leader with new innovations like own brands and the adoption of self-service shopping. The wooden counters behind which white-aproned grocers would fill housewives' baskets were soon to become museum pieces.

Failing societies transferred their businesses to stronger, larger neighbours or became part of the national Co-operative Retail Society (CRS), which had its headquarters alongside the CWS in Manchester. Although it still had the mindset of a wholesaler, the CWS also took on the role of 'ambulance', coming to the rescue of some smaller societies.

CWS loses its way

By the 1990s food retailing had been revolutionised. The two frontrunners had been joined by Asda and Morrisons and were opening more and more stores from city centre 'drop-ins' to out-of-town hypermarkets. Customers were being enticed with loyalty schemes and invited to buy their groceries online. In contrast, co-operative retailing had stood still. Despite some mergers, it was still fragmented with multiple management structures and store identities. There was no coherent brand across any more than a county or two and so national advertising was out of the question. Customer loyalty was minimal and, with a few exceptions, the link with the membership – the movement's raison d'être – had been lost.

Even the department stores, those colossal expressions of self-belief, were struggling. As town centres developed, they found themselves left behind in secondary sites, their customers driving to the out-of-town retail sheds to buy their furniture and carpets.

With falling revenues and market shares, the CWS slowly realised its future was no longer in wholesaling but in front-line retailing. It began breaking down the autonomy of the regional businesses it controlled and replacing them with national businesses. Each activity – food, pharmacies, funerals – was brought together in its own business 'silo', forcing it to see the whole picture within its individual sector. This was a positive strategic move away from regionalism but didn't go far enough.

In 1997, a hostile bid for the CWS and a subsequent damaging court case involving its executives were the spur for more radical change. The millennium saw the merger of the CWS and the CRS to create The Co-operative Group in a move than had long been predicted. Now with around 1,000 stores, the Group accounted for 80% of the co-operative retail market with assets of £32bn.

The merger and the name change set the ball rolling, at first ever so slowly. Until now each of the business 'silos' had its own support functions such as human resources and information technology. These duplications were consolidated with single functions working across each of the retail activities. A head office mentality was developing.

Rationalisation of the businesses followed. The shoe retailing, milk and creameries and engineering businesses were all sold. These were seen as distractions from the Group's core consumer interests. The large department stores also went, their repair bills overshadowing dwindling returns.

By the end of 2006, merger talks were under way with United Co-operatives, the largest remaining regional consumer co-operative in the UK serving the North West, the north Midlands and Yorkshire. It had been formed by the merger four years earlier of United Norwest and Yorkshire Co-operative Society, the former able to trace its beginnings back to the Rochdale Pioneers.

Chief Executive of United Co-operatives, Peter Marks, was already a member of The Co-operative Group's board. Marks positively supported merger and, as a shop assistant who had climbed the hierarchical ladder, was commercially motivated for the business to stay competitive through growth.

The respective Boards needed little persuasion to join forces. In July 2007 United Co-operatives ceased to exist as an independent society. The enlarged Co-operative Group was formed, with 87,500 employees, revenue of £9bn and an assertive Peter Marks as new Chief Executive.

Although steady progress was being made at the business level of the Group's activities, its Manchester property portfolio had changed little in 50 years. In a grid of streets at the northern tip of the city centre, its head office functions were spread over seven or more buildings ranging from the Hanover Building's Victorian splendour to the 1962 CIS Tower, inspired by Chicago skyscrapers and recently re-clad in 7,200 photovoltaic cells. All were architecturally acclaimed, but no longer fit for purpose.

Renovation programmes had been considered over the previous two decades and the investigation into new head office facilities even had a name – Project Granary – but previous chief executives had considered the task too complicated and had been reluctant to grasp the nettle.

Taking up his new position, Marks was appalled at the condition of the Group's estate. Cramped, old-fashioned offices, some with buckets under dripping ceilings, embodied the 'silo' mentality he was so determined to leave behind.

"If we were to be vibrant, forward-looking and competitive we had to transform the business," he recalls. "The antiquated culture had to change and, as that culture seeps through these walls, I decided we had to change the fabric of our buildings."

The CIS Tower: completed in 1962 and originally clad in 14 million pieces of mosaic, intended to resist the 'polluting Manchester air'.

The general manger reportedly commented that the reduction in office partitioning introduced in the new building was difficult to enforce because of the 'role of status in office life'.

Up sticks? As part of a thorough review of potential head office locations, these four sites around Greater Manchester were among those considered.

From top left, clockwise: a town centre site in Ashton-under-Lyne adjacent to council offices and a railway station; alongside the M60 in Oldham; a 420-acre business park off the M62 on the outskirts of Rochdale; and a compact site in the centre of Bury.

Twelve months earlier the Group had appointed a new Managing Director of Estates, responsible for over 10,000 premises around the country. Lynda Shillaw had been Group Property Director at BT and, on her arrival, had acquainted herself with the Project Granary files. In the first half of 2006, consultants had carried out a detailed survey of the Manchester buildings, so when Marks first met with Shillaw, she was able to give him an up-to-date report on Project Granary. It was not pleasant reading.

Doing nothing is not an option

Unsurprisingly, the survey showed a 'wall of cost' estimated at over £100m across the next decade just to maintain the dilapidated buildings and make them compliant with basic office standards. But the consultants had also estimated the cost of bringing the whole complex up to an efficient, modern standard taking the Group forward into the 21st century. This major refurbishment would involve temporarily relocating thousands of staff, stripping the buildings back to their cores, re-wiring, re-plumbing, re-heating and re-networking – effectively starting again from scratch. The Group was looking at a bill of up to £200m over 25 years.

"Those figures alone were enough to convince me that something had to be done," says Marks. He promoted Shillaw to the Group's Management Executive and instructed her to compile a business case to be presented to the Board.

'Doing nothing is not an option' became the rallying cry that was to lead Shillaw's property team, the Executive and ultimately the Group Board to invest in a new corporate statement that would reflect not only the new optimism and financial strength of the The Co-operative Group but also its confidence in the future of the consumer co-operative movement in the UK.

The Board agreed that a new head office was needed. Although the Group was fully occupied with a major re-branding exercise and mergers were looming with both the Somerfield supermarket chain and, later, with the Britannia Building Society, it decided to embarked on the search for a new home.

The decision was way overdue, but now it had been made, upcoming legislation would speed the process forward. Some of the existing buildings had refrigerants in their air cooling systems that would be illegal by 2013. These and other 'ticking time bombs' meant massive cost savings could be made if staff were relocated quickly.

Property consultants Jones Lang LaSalle (JJL) were commissioned to conduct a strategic site survey of all the options including relocating out of the city centre to one of the neighbouring authorities within Greater Manchester. The real possibility of moving The Co-operative Group, the city centre's largest employer, shocked many people both inside and outside the organisation.

"They had an absolute open mind and were genuinely considering moving out," recalls JJL's regional chairman, Bob Dyson. "I think, at the very beginning, it was a case of either refurbishing the existing buildings or move out of town. But there was a degree of doubt in my mind whether the Group, with its deep

The **co-operative**

Out with the old: a major rebranding exercise in 2007 signalled a reinvigorated Co-operative Group.

What might have been. In May 1993, Sir Bob Scott, Chairman of the Olympic Bid Committee, shows International Olympic Committee delegates a vision for a redeveloped Victoria Station. The bid was unsuccessful and, in the end, only the indoor arena and 'city room' were built.

association with the city, would really up sticks and relocate to Ashton, Bury, Oldham or wherever."

"At the point you are doing the evaluation, you can go anywhere you like," says Shillaw. "One argument is you go where there is the most financial assistance. Some local authorities were willing to give us land to build on and others would have paid us for every job we brought to them, but that isn't always the best argument. Clearly, if you can't take skills with you when you relocate, and you can't recruit people when you get there, then frankly you don't have a business."

Commercially-driven

After spreadsheets of figures and pages of careful analysis, the team narrowed the options down to just eight – four in Manchester city centre and four in Greater Manchester. All of them involved building a new head office on a vacant site. The brief from Marks to his property team and its advisors was unequivocal: any recommendations to the Board had to be solely for commercial reasons. Although the Group was soon to celebrate its 150th anniversary in the city, there could be no nostalgia. If Manchester as a location didn't stack up financially, the removal vans would be called in.

"My initial thoughts," recalls Marks, "were that we should go outside of Manchester. From a commercial perspective my perception was it would be cheaper to build on a greenfield site outside a major city centre. But when we started to consider all the options, the business case proved me wrong."

Parallel to the search for a new head office location, the property team was considering what was to be done with the buildings the Group was now planning to vacate. It needed to develop a strategy for the whole of its central

Manchester property portfolio and it soon became clear that this and the head office search were intertwined.

In property terms the Group's assets were immense. Few organisations could boast ownership of such a large swathe of the city centre. Despite this the northern part of the city core lay mostly undeveloped. Not only were The Co-operative's own buildings falling into disrepair, but the area around them had not benefited from the same level of regeneration as other parts of the city.

Back in 1988, a government quango, the Central Manchester Development Corporation, had been established with a 10-year remit to develop 470 acres to the south and east of the city centre. Its goals included rejuvenating waterways, stimulating home building; supporting the rebirth of the historic quarter of Castlefield and driving the development of a new international concert hall.

Meanwhile, to the north, a plan to renovate Victoria Station adjacent to The Co-operative complex was unveiled. An indoor Olympic-standard arena and office tower were planned, along with a 'city square' large enough to accommodate what the developers hoped might become a Mancunian version of Covent Garden. The Victoria Exchange project began at the end of 1992 but secured only enough funding to build the arena and a small office block. Much of the railway station remained unchanged. The arena, although a host to the Commonwealth Games rather than the Olympics, has since proved to be hugely successful and has regularly beaten London's O2 and New York's Madison Square Garden to the 'Busiest Arena Venue' title.

Despite this success, there has been a perception for many years that the city centre effectively ends where The Co-operative's estate begins. There was no need to go further north unless you were working at or visiting The Co-operative Group. Even the rebuilding following the 1996 terrorist bomb fell short of making any impact on what has been dubbed 'Co-op Land'. The derelict Maxwell House, once the northern base of media mogul Robert Maxwell and home to the largest newspaper printing complex outside London, was at the time of the detonation owned jointly by the CWS and CIS. The societies sold their asset to a Midlands-based developer which demolished all but the façade and rebuilt the interior as the cinema and entertainment complex now known as The Printworks.

With dispassionate analysis, it became clear that staying in Manchester and in close proximity to their existing base represented the best all-round deal for the Co-operative Group. If it moved away, leaving redundant, unsuitable accommodation behind, it could delay the future regeneration of the area for years to come. The 'reflective value' of a new head office adjacent to its immense property portfolio was too great an opportunity to ignore.

"This was absolutely understood by The Co-operative," says JLL's Bob Dyson. "Their new head office could become a wonderful centrepiece and act as a catalyst for the creation of a new, mixed-use community in a relatively unknown, unloved part of Manchester."

The Printworks entertainment complex: redevelopment after the terrorist bomb of 1996 effectively stopped at the border with The Co-operative's estate.

In many ways
the 'second place'
Victoria Station site
was seen as a more
straightforward
option, a self-
contained site
requiring few
infrastructure
changes.

Entrenched negotiations

So, from the eight shortlisted, two nearby sites came head to head in the final round. Neither was owned by the Group. One was at Victoria Station – owned by Network Rail – on the opposite side of Corporation Street, and the other was vacant land on Miller Street used by The Co-operative as a staff car park and owned by a Co-operative pension fund. The property team then began negotiations with both Muse Developments, Network Rail's development partner and the AXA insurance company that represented the pension fund.

Negotiations to agree terms with AXA for the purchase of its sites and Muse and Network Rail for the purchase of a bespoke building, proved very difficult and protracted. These delays frustrated the Group which had already announced to its employees that it was to stay in Manchester but, for many agonising months, was unable to announce where exactly its new head office was to be built.

In many ways the Victoria Station option was preferable. With trains, trams and an existing car park, it ticked all the boxes for connectivity; there would have been no need to expand the Group's campus, reconfigure roads or build quite so much public realm. The NOMA master plan – the name later given to The Co-operative's redevelopment scheme – would have looked very different with a reduced mix of office, retail and residential developments. But mutually acceptable terms could not be agreed and that fell through.

Stalled negotiations were then restarted with AXA and a deal was struck that saw the Miller Street site, the CIS Tower, adjoining car parks and a couple of smaller buildings come under Group ownership. Building work could now begin.

A Turbulent Past

1741

The earliest map of Manchester shows the area known as Angel Meadow to be open fields on the edge of the town. Another map, 20 years later, shows the development of properties by the apparently wealthy Roger Bradshaw and John Smith surrounded by gardens and orchards.

Richard Arkwright, often credited as the father of the modern industrial factory system, leased a former brickworks close to Angel Meadow and, with his partners, built a five-storey cotton mill. It was the first industrial-scale factory and the precursor to hundreds of textile mills in Manchester and beyond.

An archaeological survey from 2004 suggests Arkwright's original intention had been to use a steam engine to power the mill machinery but that experiment failed. Instead two reservoirs and a massive nine-metre diameter waterwheel were built and the engine, burning five tons of coal each day, was used to pump water from the lower to the upper reservoir.

Only after the mill had been sold by Arkwright did the new owner install a 40-horsepower Boulton and Watt steam engine that powered over 4,000 spindles.

The development of the mill led to the construction of houses to accommodate the workers and the naming of the adjacent road as Miller Street. Small businesses and shops appeared from the end of the 18th century to service the mill and its workers. Blakely Street (later Dantzic Street) housed a shuttle-maker, baker, butcher, block-maker and fustian-cutter, (fustian being a heavy, woven cotton used mainly for men's clothes).

1788

St Michael's Church was built adjacent to Angel Street and was planned as a 'carriage church' that wealthy Mancunians could drive to. At about the same time the Overseers of the Poor of Manchester bought land adjacent as a mass burial site.

1816

By now the burial site was full with the remains of an estimated 40,000 paupers and had become a notorious setting for cock fighting and gambling.

One local resident described the site:

'There was at one time a number of gravestones covering the remains of some dear lost ones, but these have been removed and a few are to be seen in some of the cottages... Very often are the bones of the dead exposed and carried away and a human skull has been kicked about for a football on the ground.'

In the 1850s, the whole area was flagged to prevent unscrupulous entrepreneurs digging up the graveyard and selling the soil as fertiliser to local farms. It became known as St Michael's Flags.

1835

A survey of the working classes reported that over 18,000 people – 12% of the working class population – were living in cellars in Manchester.

1845

While working in a Salford thread-making mill, the German-born social scientist and political theorist Friedrich Engels began the chronicle appalling conditions of the working classes. Guided by his lover, Mary Burns, he toured the city and documented its squalor in the influential The Condition of the Working Class in England, first published in 1845.

'If we leave the Irk and penetrate once more on the opposite side from Long Millgate into the midst of the working-men's dwellings, we shall come into a somewhat newer quarter, which stretches from St Michael's Church to Withy Grove and Shude Hill. Here, as in most of the working-men's quarters of Manchester, the pork-raisers rent the courts and build pig-pens in them. In almost every court one or even several such pens may be found, into which the inhabitants of the court throw all refuse and offal, whence the swine grow fat; and the atmosphere, confined on all four sides, is utterly corrupted by putrefying animal and vegetable substances...

'Such is the Old Town of Manchester, and on re-reading my description, I am forced to admit that instead of being exaggerated, it is far from black enough to convey a true impression of the filth, ruin and uninhabitableness, the defiance of all considerations of cleanliness, ventilation and health which characterise the construction of this single district.'

1849

Angus Reach, a London-based journalist, visited Angel Meadow in 1849 and didn't hold back with his account of the area:

'The lowest, most filthy, most unhealthy and most wicked locality in Manchester is called, singularly enough, 'Angel-meadow'. It is full of cellars and inhabited by prostitutes, their bullies, thieves, cadgers, vagrants, tramps and, in the very worst states of filth and darkness.'

1854

Arkwright's Mill, by now known as 'The Old Factory', was badly damaged by fire and its uninsured owner lost £5,000.

1863

Thirty-two-year-old Laban Baxendale founded what began as a plumbers' merchants in Hanover Street on Shudehill. Six years later, Baxendale & Co moved to new premises on Miller Street where it operated for more than 100 years.

To mark the firm's 50th anniversary in 1913, a small booklet was produced by a good friend of Baxendale's who described himself as 'an onlooker'. Noting that 1863 was, *'not a good time to start, for the cotton famine, caused by the civil war in America, was paralysing Lancashire's principal industry'*, he goes on to describe the firm's founder: *'Mr Baxendale was a man of great calmness of manner and excellent business judgement; he was seldom flurried, never excited; progressive and enterprising; frugal and polite; with a wide knowledge of the business, a man, in fact, who was naturally cut out for the position of employer. After his separation from the Church of England, he joined a small religious body known as "The Brethren," with which he remained in communion until his death. He was a cheerful and generous giver. After the firm had got fairly on its feet, and money was not so scarce, it was his habit to give freely at the factory to all and sundry. No doubt he was often imposed upon; in fact, to give wisely involves a degree of painstaking care which is but too seldom exercised. Still, many deserving cases were relieved: and it was fine to see how, as soon as he had a little money to spare, he so freely gave it away.'*

Common Lodging House
No 44 Angel Street
Room No 3
11-25 a.m. 22nd May 1897
N. Sullivan photo
CSO No 730

Page 6)				The undermentioned Houses are situate within the Boundaries of the *Parish of Royston, Cambs*						
Civil Parish [or Township] of *Royston, Cambs*	**City or Municipal Borough of**	**Municipal Ward of**	**Parliamentary Borough of**	**Town or** *Royston*	**Village or Hamlet, &c. of**	**Local Board [or Improvement Commissioners District] of**	**Ecclesiastical District of**			
No. of Schedule	ROAD, STREET, &c. and No. or NAME of HOUSE	HOUSES Inhabited	NAME and Surname of each Person	RELATION to Head of Family	CON- DITION	AGE of Males / Females	Rank, Profession, or OCCUPATION	WHERE BORN	Whether 1. Deaf-and-Dumb 2. Blind 3. Imbecile or Idiot 4. Lunatic
26	Town Yard millennium Mews	1	William Pell	Head	Mar	36	Ag. Lab	Cambs Winspol	
			Elizabeth Do	Wife	Mar		33		Do Whaddon	
			George Do	Son		17	Ag. Lab	Do Orwell	
			John Do	Do		14	Do	Do Do	
			Harry Do	Do		9	Scholar	Do Do	
			Susanna Do	Daur		5	Do	Do Whaddon	
			Anne Maria Do	Do		1		Do Royston	
27		1	William Strader	Head	Unm	49	Wholesale Draper, Linen & Boys	Do Do	
			Mary Do	Mother	W	72	Annuitant	Hunts Royston	
			Ann Do	Sister	Unm	44	Schoolmistress	Hunts Do	
			Sarah Do	Do	Unm	62	Authoress	Hunts Do	
			Eleanor Do	Do	Unm	43	Authoress	Do Do	
			Harriet Do	Do	Unm	31	no Profession	Do Do	
			Charlotte Howes	Serv	Unm	27	General Serv (Domestic)	Cambs Bassingbourn	
28		1	Henry Thurnall	Head	Mar	42	Attorney & Landowner	Cambs Oxford	

1870–71

For a series of articles in the Manchester Guardian, a reporter made several trips to the area and was horrified to find conditions had worsened since Engels' report 25 years earlier.

Following the potato famine of 1845–52 Angel Meadow, as the cheapest part of town, became a popular destination for Irish immigrants. Cellar living was prevalent and it seems there was nowhere that was deemed unsuitable for accommodation.

'On the other side of the court there appeared to be no habitation, or anything that could ever have been such. There was an outhouse, with a window in which six out of the eight panes were stuffed with rags, but it was evident that there could be nobody living there. One of the neighbours, however, said it was inhabited, and so it proved. The door opened into a room about seven feet square, filthy, and in such a state of utter neglect and disrepair that one might suppose even a rat would leave it. The staircase was scarcely safe to venture on, and led to another room of the same size and character, with the roof in such a state that the rain penetrated not only into it, but down through the wretched flooring into the next. Immediately outside what was formerly the window stood the privy of the neighbourhood. The dwelling was inhabited by a woman and her boy.'

1870s

Many of the larger houses in the district, originally built for wealthy families, were by now occupied by two or more families or converted into lodging houses where three pence a night would buy a half share of a bed, the sleeping partners determined on a first-come first-served basis.

1890s

The lodging houses around Angel Meadow were notoriously used for prostitution, prompting the Reverend of St Michael's Church to claim, *'The class of fallen women is very large and aggressive. Of the 42 streets of the parish, only 18 can be said to be free from this class (prostitutes), and many of these 18 even are doubtful. The following figures will give some idea of the state of the two principal streets. Angel Street, with 54 houses, has only eight quite free. Charter Street, with 79 houses, has only 21 quite free. Further, there are 15 lodging houses which are practically quite given up to this class of women, and a large number lodge in the mixed lodging houses with the men who live on their earnings.'*

1892

Baxendale & Co Ltd, the plumber's merchant and engineering company, bought the fire-damaged 'Old Factory' and redeveloped the surrounding site.

1940

Much of the decaying housing stock was demolished through slum clearances before the Second World War, leaving the remaining buildings on Miller Street to be severely damaged or destroyed in the Manchester Blitz of 1940.

The Manchester Town Planning Committee continued what the Luftwaffe had begun and compulsory purchased and demolished much of what was left apart from Baxendales who rebuilt their offices and celebrated their centenary in 1963 on Miller Street.

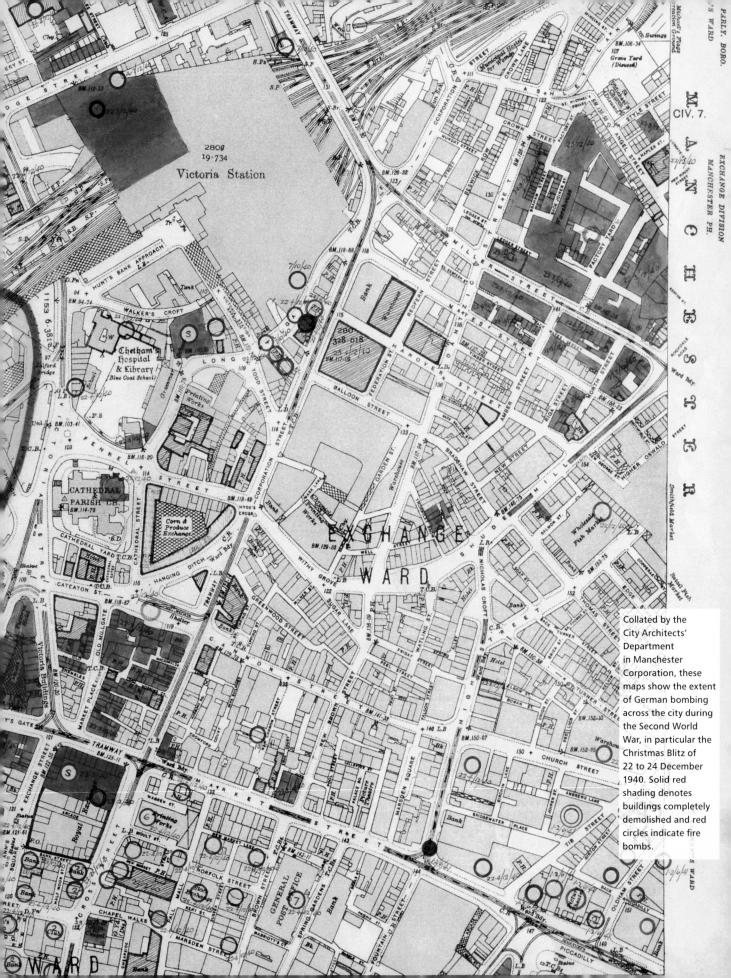

Collated by the City Architects' Department in Manchester Corporation, these maps show the extent of German bombing across the city during the Second World War, in particular the Christmas Blitz of 22 to 24 December 1940. Solid red shading denotes buildings completely demolished and red circles indicate fire bombs.

1960s

Baxendale and Co Ltd in 1964 (above), with the nearly completed New Century House on the left and the CIS Tower on the right.

2009

Oxford Archaeology North (OAN) was commissioned by The Co-operative Group in June 2009 to conduct an archaeological dig on the site of the new head office. The excavations revealed good examples of the type of housing that Engels might have encountered while researching his treatise on the living conditions of Manchester's working poor.

OAN Project Officer Chris Wild says the area would have developed in the latter part of the 18th century, with wide open streets and large merchant houses overlooking Red Bank. By the 1820s the area would have been crammed, with every available space filled with one building or another and the wealthy merchants long gone.

"Our test trenches revealed that the area where we might have expected to find good remains had actually been destroyed by later activity. It was only around the edges, along the main street frontages, that we found extant examples.

"We excavated the remains of cellars on Charter Street and Angel Street, found outbuildings, wells and back yards. Out of 75 structures unearthed it was encouraging to find examples of true back-to-back housing from that period as it's something that, surprisingly, we don't see that often. And the larger houses converted to lodging houses – we hadn't uncovered any of these before."

The OAN team found numerous artifacts during their dig: 1,628 pieces of pottery; 355 remnants of clay tobacco pipe; 42 coins, including a half crown from 1885; and 84 animal bones. Most of the 762 pieces of glass discovered were from bottles, including Co-op milk bottles. Even the labels on the gin and beer bottles were revealing. "Local brewers clearly covered a huge population in a small geographical area," continues Wild, "and so we found different bottles here than we'd uncover in nearby Ancoats or Salford.

"The dig massively increased our understanding of domestic life in that time and has helped us build a better picture of the topography of workers' dwellings in Manchester and Salford."

2010

In January 2010, the discovery of a human skeleton unearthed on the Miller Street site lead to a murder enquiry. The victim had been wrapped up in carpet off-cuts and dumped alongside a hoarding, where she was found by one of the workmen. She had suffered a fractured collarbone, jawbone and neck. The police confirmed that she had died some time between 1975 and 1988.

Forensic anthropologists subsequently produced a facial reconstruction and a sustained media campaign was launched. Three years on from the discovery the police have not identified the victim but believe she may have been a foreign national.

Beyond the Beehive

When a 39-year-old Glaswegian architect stepped off the train at Manchester Piccadilly in 2005, he could never have imagined that within four years he and his colleagues would be designing the most prestigious architectural commission in North West England.

Jim Webster, a director with one of Scotland's leading practices, 3D Architects, had been sent south to set up a regional office but was not optimistic about breaking into an established market. "Manchester is a very knowledgeable city and was already full of very good architectural practices," he recalls. "Although 3D was well known north of the border, we only had a fairly average portfolio. There was nothing spectacular to show potential clients."

Working at first out of the spare bedroom in his city centre apartment, recruiting staff and searching for premises, Webster knew only one other person in Manchester's commercial property community. Planning consultant Ruairidh Jackson had stepped off the same train a month or so earlier to take up the position of Planning Manger at The Co-operative Group.

The pair had worked together in Glasgow and Jackson, aware of Webster's capabilities, invited him to examine the development scope for some of the smaller properties in the Group's considerable portfolio.

The emerging Manchester office cut its teeth on what Webster describes as "run-of-the-mill commercial work" for The Co-operative Group before being invited to design the conversion of a Victorian shoe factory in Leicester. "Jim designed a really tidy residential scheme," says Jackson, "but we then sold the building as part of the Group's rationalisation programme."

Having proved its credentials the practice was invited to join the property team in preparing its latest study into the long-term viability of The Co-operative's existing estate.

Webster had recently recruited Mike Hitchmough from Manchester-based developer, Dandara. Hitchmough recalls the analysis: "We worked with The Co-operative to examine how much it would cost the Group to stay in its existing listed buildings for the next 25 years. That included replacing windows, roofs, escalators, lifts, all the electrical and networking equipment, everything. The cost of remaining in the existing premises came to nearly £200m, which was more than the cost of building a new head office. The business case was clear for all to see."

As the Group's newly appointed Managing Director of Estates Lynda Shillaw and its Director of Investment and Property Strategy David Pringle began to prepare a business case for the creation of a new head office, a parallel plan emerged. Whatever happened with the head office, it was apparent that the Group would be vacating thousands of square feet of prime office space and a master plan was needed to help shape future developments.

The bigger prize

By this time, 3D Architects had merged with Reid Architecture and the resulting 3DReid had shot into the UK's architectural top 10 with offices in Birmingham, London, Glasgow, Edinburgh and the Middle East and turnover in excess of £20m. But despite this backing, Webster was cautious.

The existing estate: disparate head office functions split over numerous locations in sub-standard accommodation.

"We'd established a good reputation by then and some of my colleagues were keen to bid for the master plan," he says. "But I was aware the competition would be tough and our limited portfolio was unlikely to see us through."

With an eye on the bigger prize Webster and his team decided not to enter the international competition for the master plan and were instead appointed by the Group as advisors. Webster helped organise the competition, compiled a shortlist and sat alongside the panel judges to assess the presentations.

A joint venture of commercial property agents Jones Lang LaSalle and the engineering and design consultancy Arup won the master plan competition and drew up a scheme for the 20-acre development that would effectively create a new commercially led destination in the city. In March 2008, Manchester City Council confirmed a £20m contribution to the Group's plans for new public spaces that would at last link the 'Co-op Quarter' to the city centre. Seen by some as a 'sweetener' to stay put, the council's contribution was a shrewd investment. Had the Group moved out of town the council might have been faced with a much larger financial incentive to entice an incoming developer to take on deserted buildings too easily overtaken with tumbleweed.

It was another year before the local authority officially approved the master plan as a 'strategic planning framework' and another two before the plan was refined, branded and launched to the property community in March 2011 as the £800m NOMA development.

Webster's strategy paid off. With the master planning team beginning to look at the wider picture, the Group offered 3DReid the opportunity to come up with some designs for a head office.

"The original brief filled just half a page of A4," recalls Webster. "They wanted a total of 250,000 sq ft with floor plates of a minimum of 20,000 sq ft. It was to be low carbon; close to a transport hub; and it had to have the highest BREEAM rating. That was effectively the brief. The idea of flexible working came later."

The Building Research Establishment Environmental Assessment Method (BREEAM) is an international standard for sustainable design and a building's environmental performance. Over the next few years, the desire to achieve BREEAM 'outstanding' status was to focus the minds and test the technical skills of the entire design team.

3DReid set about assessing the Group's requirements and visited each of the departments that would eventually come together under one roof. "The head office functions were split over more than 60 floors across seven or eight city centre buildings," says Webster. "We spoke to all the department heads and built up an overview of their requirements: staff numbers, storage needs, departments within departments, front of house, post rooms, deliveries, everything was considered."

Co-operative inspiration

Meanwhile, Hitchmough was drawing inspiration for the form of the building from the architectural history of the co-operative movement. "They took great pride in their buildings," he says, "every town centre had a grand Co-op building that was an urban and social focal point. The Manchester estate is testament to the movement's commitment to building design and each of the buildings was a perfect architectural manifestation of the period in which it was conceived. The attention to detail was quite phenomenal."

3DReid's research identified past symbolism used by the movement, often embodied by elements that were sculpted into the fabric of the buildings themselves.

"The wheatsheaf and the beehive are recurring symbols that represent collective strength," Hitchmough says. "One strand of wheat cannot stand on its own but, if many strands are bound together, there is enormous strength. The beehive, too, symbolises the power of collective work towards a common goal, and we wanted to find a way of embedding these founding principles into the very heart of the building."

Although the curve of the wheatsheaf can be seen in some of 3DReid's earliest designs – and has, indeed, been carried through into the final shape – it was the beehive, or more precisely the wasps' nest, that became the inspiration for Hitchmough's preferred design. "The 'skeps' as they are traditionally called, started out as old, upturned baskets," he explains. "The concentric spiral of straw or grass bound together with stronger, thinner ties weaving in and out gave us the image we were looking for."

Co-operative symbols
of collaboration,
unity and strength,
the wheatsheaf
and the beehive
become important
visual references for
architects, 3DReid.

But it's not just pattern for pattern's sake. The vertical elements that represent the strong binding ties in the beehive design also act as solar shading devices and so had a function that contributed towards the building's sustainability targets. "Although the fluid form of the building is in stark contrast to the angular Miller Street tower, we wanted to create a visual connection with it. The external fins – the shading devices – echo those on the tower."

By mid-2008, having worked though a number of different scenarios, 3DReid's 'beehive' concept had been well received and Webster felt they had given the client the building they needed. The Group appointed other members of the team – Gardiner & Theobald as cost and project managers and Buro Happold as mechanical and structural engineering consultants – and so it seemed the project was moving forward. Then, almost as soon as the Group had announced its intention to stay in Manchester, everything went quiet. Design was put on hold and momentum lost as the property team entered prolonged, frustrating negotiations over the two potential development sites on their doorstep.

Although disheartening for the architects, these months of inactivity in the second half of 2008 gave the team a breather before the next phase of design mayhem that would see the 'beehive' change radically.

On 13th January, 2009 Webster and Hitchmough were called to a meeting in David Pringle's office. "I've got some good news and some bad news," he'd said.

"I told them we had secured the Miller Street site and that they were being given the opportunity of designing our new head office. The bad news, for them, was that I needed not one, but three design concepts to take to the Board in a matter of weeks."

Walking back to their offices, Webster and Hitchmough had two very different reactions to the news. "Jim was overflowing with enthusiasm because we were being given the chance to design The Co-operative's new headquarters," recalls Hitchmough. "You have to remember that a few months earlier, Lehman Brothers had collapsed and a financial crisis was looming, and here was our fledgling company on the verge of a major commission that would see us through."

While still appreciating the positive commercial implications, Hitchmough's mind was on the 'beehive' design. "I was completely distraught," he says. "I couldn't see any way we could improve on the design we already had. And yet we were being asked to come up with more solutions."

The pressure was suddenly on again. Now a decision had been reached to build on Miller Street, a deadline was set and schedules were determined by Group Board meetings and the City Council's planning meetings.

Designing at speed

"We drafted in the help of our other offices," says Hitchmough. "The London office were working on it, staff from our Glasgow office came to Manchester to develop ideas and of course our own team were flat out too. It was seven days a week, full-on."

Essential for efficient air circulation and environmental control, the atrium also acts as the 'social glue' that binds the head office functions together, reinforcing the co-operative movement's core values and principles. This visualisation, from an early concept design booklet produced by 3DReid in mid-2008, also includes a network of bridges to 'encourage open and clear communication and teamwork between employees'.

By the end of 2008 the Miller Street site – a car park opposite the CIS Tower – had been confirmed as the preferred site. It would effectively extend the city centre boundary further north.

Five or six new solutions were worked up in the weeks that followed. Some barely got off the computer screen. "One was for a straightforward tower, but that didn't get past first base," says Hitchmough. "'We've got a tower,' they said. 'Why do we need another one?'"

Although convinced the 'beehive' couldn't be improved upon, Hitchmough and his colleagues knew they had to give the design another long, hard look and assess its weaknesses as well as its strengths. Flexibility became the focus. The original brief, albeit short, had made flexibility a priority and the Group saw this as a future asset. It was conceivable that, in a few decades' time, and with radically different working practices, a 15-storey city centre head office would no longer match the Group's business model. Even before the foundations had been dug, the Group was considering how attractive its new head office might be in any future commercial marketplace.

The 'beehive' wasn't as flexible as the design team would have liked. They struggled with the optimum location of the lift cores, at one point having a lift shaft at the 'nose' of the building, which negated the aspiration for people to be able to see into the building and view the activity inside.

"Aesthetically it was very pleasing, but it wasn't such a sensible design in commercial terms," says Pringle. "It might have been fine for us now but it didn't have the longevity we were looking for."

3DReid consulted again with the client's hard-nosed property agents, Bob Dyson of Jones Lang LaSalle and Mike Hawkins at WHR Property Consultants, who advised on the commercial viability of the designs.

"We made flexibility our starting point," recalls Hitchmough, "and came up with a series of three buildings of differing heights, configured in a triangle and joined at the corners." Each component had its own entrance and so could potentially be used by three different occupiers. The scheme, known as the 'agent' because of the property consultants' input, ticked all the boxes for flexibility but was rejected by Pringle as being too disparate.

"There is a limit to the amount of flexibility you can build into an office block of that magnitude," says Dyson. "Our job, at the end of the day, was to bring a commercial overlay to the design and make sure that the value – now and in the future – was enhanced."

The design team then began to modify the design yet again, blending the three elements together, to create one entrance, and give the building a single identity. At the same time Hitchmough reoriented the building so it tilted due south, allowing for maximum solar gain during the winter. And then, with an eye to its proximity to a nearby residential block, he 'pushed the front of the building down' which, to maintain the overall floor area, meant the back of the building had to rise up, creating a raked effect. Those working on the upper floors would then have direct views out across the city and benefit from maximum daylight, adding to the building's BREEAM ratings.

After weeks of frenetic activity three designs were presented to the Board (top to bottom): the 'winter garden', the 'beehive' and the 'star', known around 3DReid's office as the 'X factor'.

With its stepped upper floors and a series of double-height breakout spaces at each corner, this new design became known as the 'winter garden'. It retained the skep patterning of the beehive design, and the curved atrium made a subtle reference to the wheatsheaf inspiration.

"The 'beehive' was a good building but once the 'winter garden' design started to come together we felt it was much better in terms of functionality and flexibility," says Hitchmough. "But both were quite fluid and organic and, as part of our presentation to the Board, we felt we had an obligation to offer a more conventional office building, at least as an option. So we came up with the 'X factor', as we called it around the office, due to its plan form, but known as the 'star' for our presentation."

With a blending and rounding of the edges the 'agent' scheme morphed from three distinct blocks into one homogenous shape that eventually became the 'winter garden'.

The 'X factor' was developed in parallel with the other two options and was seen very much as a fallback option in case the Board thought the other two designs were too unconventional. Its position as number three in the presentation document perhaps signified the project architect's ambivalence towards it. But its inclusion reflected the practice's nervousness: even at this point in the design process 3DReid had not been officially commissioned.

"Although we felt that we were performing well, our position wasn't secure. For all we knew, there might well have been another practice working up alternative schemes in parallel to ours," says Hitchmough. "We just didn't know and couldn't take any chances. We pulled out all the stops to make sure the client was delighted with everything we did at every stage."

Hitchmough needn't have worried. Pringle says the Group Board did consider whether an international competition should be launched to select an architect for such a significant new building. But the property team was not in favour. Apart from the expense, the in-house professionals were concerned that the ego of a 'signature architect' would be incompatible with the Group's values and principles and get in the way of the all-important functionality.

"Jim and Mike had worked closely with us over the previous two years and had spent a lot of time getting to know the organisation and what made us tick," says Pringle. "We'd built up a strong relationship and a mutual trust with 3DReid. They understood us."

Faced with the prospect of taking an additional six months to run a competition and having been convinced of 3DReid's commitment, the Board accepted Pringle's recommendation and kept the programme on track.

Now, at the beginning of March, seven weeks after their January meeting the architects had three designs worked up and ready to be presented to the Group Board.

Looking back, Hitchmough is pragmatic about the demise of the 'beehive' and its evolution into the 'winter garden'. "I suppose, in a perverse way, we have to be thankful to David and Lynda for making our lives hell for several months! If they hadn't challenged us to go away and think again, then we wouldn't have come up with the building we have now."

Pringle is also happy with the way the process resulted in a better solution. "From a purely commercial pointed view it was always going to be a winner. Each of the floors could split into separate units of between 3,000 and 8,000 sq ft, all with their own front doors, which suited the Manchester market. So in terms of onward flexibility, it was brilliant and none of the other designs came close."

Final approval

3DReid presented the schemes to the Group's Executive on the 9th March, 2009. "They had a sneak preview before the Board meeting scheduled for the end of the month," says Hitchmough, "and at the end of that meeting, although nothing was said, we had a pretty good feeling the 'winter garden' was their favourite too."

But it was only the Board that could give final approval and the next meeting was not until the 30th March. The design team – the architects, engineers, project managers and surveyors – were faced with a dilemma. If the tight schedule was to be met then detailed drawings had to be submitted to the City Council's planning meeting in July. If the team waited until the Board meeting's decision, there would be insufficient time to finalise the drawings. So, unknown to their client, the team took a flyer and started to work up plans for the 'winter garden' at their own expense, hoping it would be selected by the Board.

For the Board that month's meeting was the culmination of 18 months of discussion about the new head office. Ever since Shillaw had presented the business case back in 2007, the Board had made incremental decisions about its development. Group Secretary Moira Lees explains the process: "At first the Board agreed that something had to be done about a new head office and authorised the Executive to investigate the options. Next, a case was presented for the Group to stay in Manchester and the board had agreed. Then site assembly, design parameters and so on."

By the March meeting the Board had travelled a long journey with the Group's senior management and its team of consultants. It was already familiar with the 'beehive' design and knew how it fulfilled the Group's requirements. It understood the need for the building to be 'future-proofed', how a large atrium facilitated fresh air circulation and why extra investment was needed for a biomass boiler. This presentation would push them all over the line, arriving at a consensus that the 'winter garden' was the preferred option and effectively securing 3DReid's commission.

The Group's Chief Executive, Peter Marks, recalls the meeting: "We had a very free and open discussion and it was clear that the majority of people were moving in that direction. To be honest, I am not very good at design. I am a commercial animal, more interested in what the building could do for our organisation, what it would cost and where the money was coming from. There are others in the Group who were far better at assessing architectural merit. But we liked what 3DReid had brought to the table. They won it purely on the ideas they had."

A month later, the Executive, having finalised the construction costs, brought its budget to the Board for final approval. In the meantime there had been a governance review. Half the Board members were new and therefore unfamiliar with the journey so far. "The new Board started to ask questions and queried the expenditure," explains Lees. "This was a dynamic we hadn't anticipated and it caused major palpitations within the property team. So we went through the process again, explaining why we were doing it, and eventually got the approval that everyone had expected to be a formality."

European expertise

While the concept design was being approved, the Group's property team was searching for a contractor to build its first city centre office building since the CIS Tower was completed 50 years earlier.

> "We gave it quite a distinctive form that made it sit quietly confident on the skyline rather than being big and brash for the sake of it."
>
> Mike Hitchmough, 3DReid.

The team and their consultants identified seven construction companies which they considered capable of taking on what some commentators were describing as the largest construction contract outside South East England.

Not all builders are the same and so each contender was required to complete an industry-standard questionnaire allowing the client to compare their financial stability and technical suitability for the job. Once their responses had been independently scored against a series of selection criteria, four were invited to formally pitch in the first of a two-stage process.

BAM Construction was not a natural front-runner. The competition was tight and there were more experienced, longer-established firms on the shortlist. BAM's Commercial Director, Ian Fleming thought his company, although not possibly perceived by the client as being in the top division, could be in with a chance at winning this prestigious project from under the noses of the 'big project boys'. "We realised we had a steep hill to climb if we were to get on the shortlist," he says. "We had to impress the client with our European experience."

BAM Construction is a subsidiary of Royal BAM, the largest construction company in Holland and one of the biggest in Europe. Its presence in the UK is relatively recent having bought HBG in 2002. In turn, HBG had brought together a number of smaller, although well-established construction firms including Higgs and Hill. Royal BAM's UK acquisitions also included the veteran construction and civil engineering company, Edmund Nuttall, which was later renamed BAM Nuttall. Established in Manchester in 1865, Nuttalls was involved in major projects such as the Manchester Ship Canal (opened in 1894) and the construction of the Liver Building in 1911 on Liverpool's waterfront.

So although BAM didn't have a particularly strong UK portfolio in its own name it was the company's international reputation that would see it through. Royal BAM had built the Palais Quartier in Frankfurt and head offices for Shell in the Hague and for ING in Amsterdam, and were, at the time, completing high profile football stadiums in South Africa for the forthcoming World Cup.

ING's head office in Amsterdam was just one of Royal BAM's recent high profile contracts that reinforced its European expertise.

3DReid's challenging design was certainly not beyond the capabilities of any of the competing contractors but there were elements – like the roof and façade detail and some of the environmental technologies – that were more commonplace in Europe than in the UK. In their favour, Fleming's team had the expertise of their European colleagues to draw on.

To help pull the first stage bid together Fleming drew on the experience of Tony Grindrod, a senior construction manager who had been with the company since 2001 and was well known for his hands-on approach to project management. At the time he was coordinating, among other schemes, the construction of a college in Merseyside but Fleming saw him as the one who, if they were successful, would lead on the company's most prestigious contract.

After the first stage – during which each contractor had to price its overheads and state the level of profit it was hoping to make – the BAM team attended another interview at New Century House.

"I immediately felt hopeful because this time, as we sat down, we were offered sandwiches!" recalls Fleming. "That's usually an indication that things are looking good. They didn't tell us there and then but the mood was very positive."

Fleming's assessment proved right. The Group's Programme Director for the new building, Peter Cookson, phoned the next week to pass on the good news: BAM was the only contractor chosen to move on to stage two, working with the client and design team to develop and cost the project. It was the favoured bidder but still had some way to go before crossing the finishing line.

"By this point in the process I had to pass on my other commitments," recalls Grindrod, "and start working intensively with the rest of the project team. Although the design was agreed we had the complex challenge of deciding how we were going to build it and how long that might take."

Cookson says: "We split the construction work into two packages. Before the main contract got under way we commissioned BAM to undertake the £2m 'enabling works', preparing the land and constructing the foundations. We didn't want to nail our colours to the mast too soon. It gave us time to continue negotiations over individual contracts in the main contract and to assess BAM's capabilities."

At the beginning of 2010, after the team from Oxford Archeology North had completed their investigations, BAM installed its green cabins and began preparing the site. As workmen began removing an old wooden hoarding they made a discovery more sensational than any the archeologists had made. A subsequent police report stated: 'The remains of a woman were discovered on Monday 25 January 2010, by workers preparing an area known as Angel Meadows between Angel Street, Dantzic Street and Miller Street for redevelopment.' The police later stated the woman, thought to be aged between 18 and 30, had been murdered some time in the 1970s or 1980s. Media appeals – including a feature on the BBC Crimewatch programme – and facial reconstructions have failed to identify the woman since dubbed the 'Angel of the Meadow'.

The gruesome discovery failed to divert BAM from its task of site preparation as the team continued to work with their new partners on sub-contractor negotiations. "We got a good idea of BAM's competence during this period," recalls Cookson. "You could see how well they were running their site and their attitude to the local community."

However, the Group's property team had still not fully committed themselves. "The advantage of the two-stage tendering process and splitting off the first phase of construction was that there was still time – if we were unhappy with our first choice contractor – to jump ship and engage someone else," says Cookson.

For Grindrod and Fleming there was an anxious wait. "It's not unknown for a client to switch contractors late in the day," says Grindrod. "But no one else was working on the second stage bid so they must have felt pretty confident in our approach by then."

BAM passed the test, and in June 2010 was officially appointed as contractors for the new head office and on 16th July construction began.

"The 'silver spade in the ground' photocall was great. You just felt this was a once-in-a-lifetime opportunity," says Jim Webster (far right) with (left to right), Mike Hitchmough, Peter Marks and The Co-operative Group Chair, Len Wardle.

"IT'S GOING TO BE SUCH AN ENVIRONMENTALLY ENHANCED BUILDING, AND SUCH A HANDSOME BUILDING... EVERYONE IS REALLY ENTHUSIASTIC ABOUT BEING INVOLVED.

OUR JOB BECOMES THAT MUCH
EASIER ON A SCHEME OF THIS
ILK DUE TO THE EXCITEMENT
THE PROJECT CREATES."

TONY GRINDROD
CONSTRUCTION MANAGER,
BAM CONSTRUCTION LTD

"THE SNOW THAT
WINTER HAD BEEN
HORRENDOUS
AND WE WERE
BEHIND BY THREE
WEEKS DUE TO
THE WEATHER.
HOWEVER, WE
SPOTTED AN
OPPORTUNITY
TO START THE
STEELWORK WHILE
WE WERE STILL
STRIKING THE
SLIPFORM – THE
SLIDING 'MOULDS'
FOR THE CONCRETE
CORES – AND
SO WE WERE
ABLE TO GET
OURSELVES BACK
ON PROGRAMME
BY USING THIS AND
SOME EXTENDED
WORKING."

"FIRST WE WOULD INSTALL THE STEEL IN ONE SECTION AND, AS WE MOVED ON TO THE NEXT SECTION AT THAT LEVEL, WE'D LIFT THE PRE-CAST FLOOR SLABS INTO THE FIRST SECTION FOLLOWED BY THE STRUCTURAL SCREED."

"BY THEN WE'D BE READY FOR THE NEXT LEVEL OF STEEL.
SO IT WOULD BE STEEL, SLAB, SCREED, STEEL, SLAB, SCREED,
SPIRALLING UP THE BUILDING."

"BY GETTING AS MUCH THERMAL MASS INTO THE BUILDING – IN THIS CASE, CONCRETE –
WE ARE PROVIDING A SPONGE TO ABSORB WARM AIR. THE WARM AIR RISES,
HITS THE CONCRETE CEILING, AND IS ABSORBED INTO THE CEILING."

"IT'S ALL ABOUT THE ACCURACY OF THE STRUCTURE ONTO WHICH YOU'RE INSTALLING THE STEEL. ON THIS BUILDING THE STEELWORK SPRUNG OFF THE GROUND FLOOR SLAB AND WRAPPED AROUND THE THREE CORES, ALL OF WHICH HAD STEELWORK CAST INTO THEM. SO IF ALL THAT'S ACCURATE THEN THE PROCESS IS NOT DIFFICULT. IT WENT UP SWEETLY."

"AS WELL AS ALLOWING US TO WORK ON THE ATRIUM SPACE ITSELF THE SCAFFOLDING ALSO ACTED AS A ROOF STRUCTURE AS WE INSTALLED THE PERMANENT ROOF. SO AT THE 11TH FLOOR IT SPANNED THE WHOLE ATRIUM AND KEPT THE REST OF THE BUILDING WEATHERTIGHT. OFF THAT WE ERECTED AN ACCESS SCAFFOLD TO COMPLETE THE ROOF STRUCTURE."

"IT WILL BE AN ICONIC
BUILDING BUT THAT IN ITSELF
IS QUITE A BALANCE.
THE BUILDING IS SYMBOLIC
OF THE CO-OPERATIVE'S
REJUVENATION,
BUT WE CAN'T BE SEEN
TO BE INDULGENT."

Sept 2011

RATHER THAN MONOPOLISE THE BUSY TOWER CRANES THE INSIDE
WINDOW PANELS WERE INSTALLED BY A SMALL TEAM OF 'SPIDER CRANES'
POSITIONED ON THE FLOORS ABOVE. "WE'D HOPED TO INSTALL THESE PANELS
USING A MONORAIL BUT WE FOUND THAT IT WASN'T FAST ENOUGH SO THEY
WERE NEARLY ALL PUT IN PLACE WITH SPIDER CRANES."

Nov 2011

"IT HAS BEEN DESIGNED
DOWN TO THE MILLIMETRE,
IT HAS BEEN FABRICATED
DOWN TO THE MILLIMETRE,
IT HAS BEEN SURVEYED
DOWN TO THE MILLIMETRE.
SO YES, ONCE IT'S LIFTED
INTO THE AIR, WE KNOW
IT'S GOING TO FIT."

"WE'LL BE MOVING FROM ABOUT 1,000,000 SQ FT TO 350,000 SQ FT
SO THE SAME NUMBER OF PEOPLE WILL BE IN A THIRD OF THE SPACE."

"IT'S MORE THAN A PIECE OF ARCHITECTURE. IT'S ACTUALLY
THE CO-OPERATIVE MAKING A STATEMENT ABOUT WHERE IT SEES ITSELF."

"IT'S A TIGHT PROGRAMME AND A COMPLICATED BUILDING, SO WE'VE HAD TO START THE MECHANICAL AND

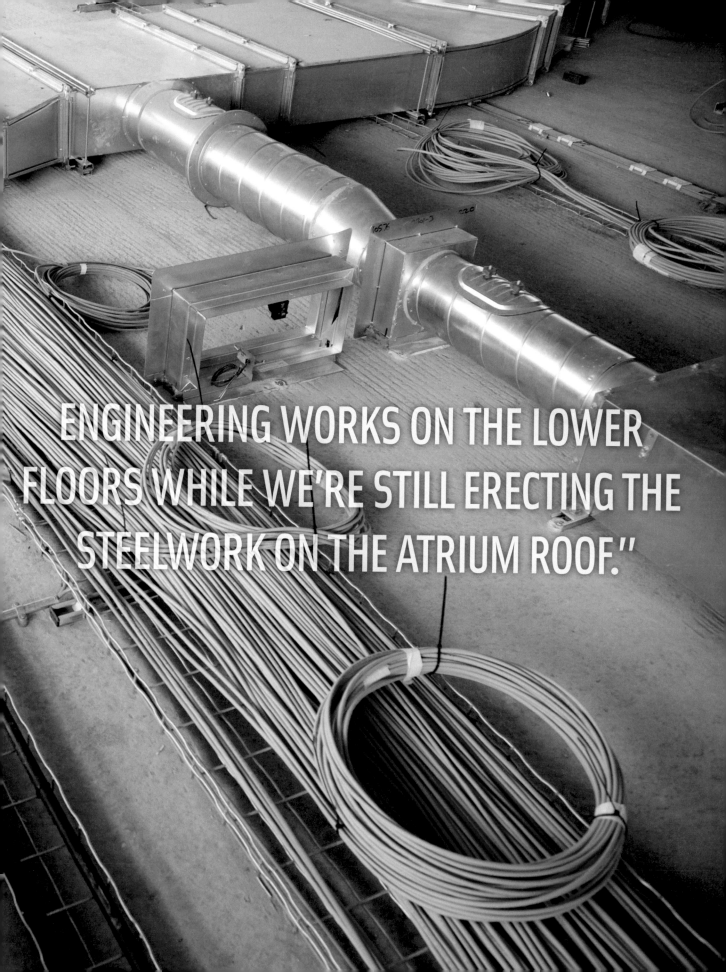

ENGINEERING WORKS ON THE LOWER
FLOORS WHILE WE'RE STILL ERECTING THE
STEELWORK ON THE ATRIUM ROOF."

Pragmatic Innovation

With its goal of becoming the most sustainable business in the UK, was there ever any doubt that a new head office building for The Co-operative Group would be at the forefront of environmental sustainability?

The original brief to the architects might have been short but it was very specific. As well as having adaptable floor plates and being close to a transport hub, the new building had to be carbon neutral, reach the highest possible industry standard for sustainability and achieve top marks for energy efficiency.

"For The Co-operative these targets were never add-on aspirations," says architect Mike Hitchmough. "They were written into the contracts of both the design team and the contractor. With the client, we have a joint responsibility to ensure those targets are met. We're all in it together."

However, the client was not insisting on sustainability at any cost. There was no blank cheque. Just as a solid commercial business case had to be made for staying in central Manchester, the extra investment committed to the head office's 'green' credentials had to be justifiable. Moving from draughty, inefficient old buildings and making significant savings on heat and power was part of the business case, but so was the inclusion of the most up-to-date technologies available. The Group was effectively future-proofing its investment by getting ahead in the property market – this way, it would take longer for 1 Angel Square to become obsolete.

Also, as phase one in a new £800m city centre neighbourhood, 1 Angel Square would become a marker for the rest of NOMA. Everything that followed had to at least match the head office's environmental achievements.

Although it had to be at the cutting edge, the Group could not afford its new head office to be a guinea pig for untested technologies. The idea of relocating hundreds of staff to a new building where the heating didn't work was unappealing.

"Europe is about 10 years ahead of the UK in environmental technologies," says NOMA director David Pringle. "If we could transfer some of those tried and tested technologies to our situation then we wouldn't have to re-invent the wheel."

Pringle called his approach "pragmatic innovation". It was this philosophy of bringing together a large number of established initiatives into one building that would focus the design team.

"There are plenty of buildings that show off their 'eco bling'," says Hitchmough, "a prominent wind turbine here and a row of photovoltaic cells there. But here we're combining genuine environmental features – rather than token gestures – that will reach the highest possible standards set by the industry."

A team led by Nigel Holden, The Co-operative's Head of Energy and Environment, is at the forefront of energy conservation for this multi-billion pound retail business. With energy costs in excess of £100m a year across the whole Group, even the smallest incremental savings are significant. In 2007,

Unwilling for its new head office to be a guinea pig for environmental experimentation, The Co-operative Group has packed the building with proven innovations.

The final design was tested against predicted 2050 weather data to ensure it had the resilience to cope with climate change.

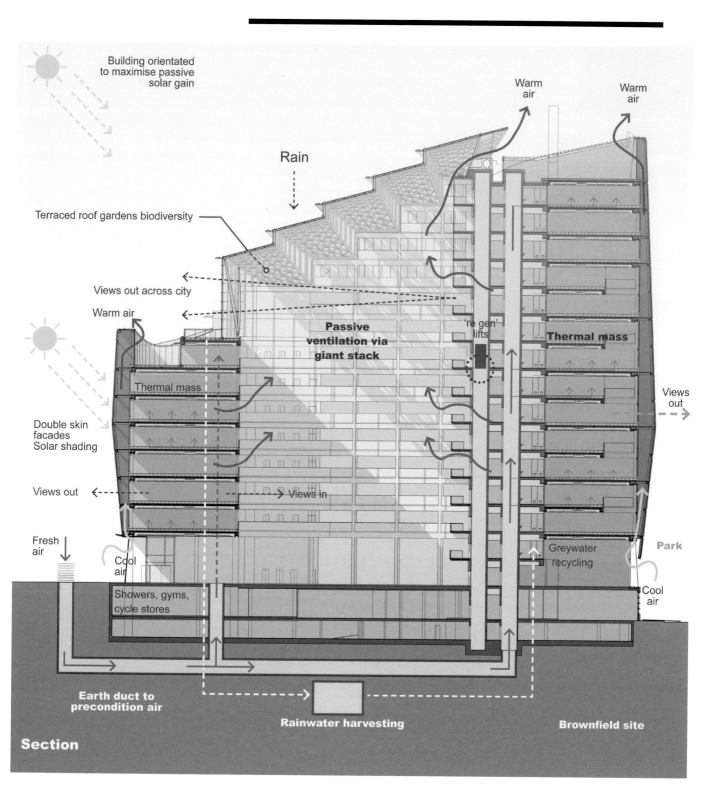

Building orientated to maximise passive solar gain

Rain

Terraced roof gardens biodiversity

Warm air

Warm air

Views out across city

Warm air

're gen' lifts

Thermal mass

Passive ventilation via giant stack

Thermal mass

Double skin facades Solar shading

Views out

Views in

Views out

Fresh air

Cool air

Showers, gyms, cycle stores

Greywater recycling

Park

Cool air

Earth duct to precondition air

Rainwater harvesting

Brownfield site

Section

Holden's team embarked on an ambitious five-year programme to reduce energy consumption by 25%, primarily across the Group's food business – stores and transportation – and its plethora of warehouses and offices. This target was achieved within four years. At the beginning of 2012 a new target was set, this time to reduce carbon emissions by 50% across the Group by 2020, and it was against this backdrop of environmental efficiency that 1 Angel Square was designed and built.

"Yes, we could have built it more cheaply," agrees Holden. "And, if we'd not been concerned about our carbon footprint, we could operate it at a lower ongoing cost. But in reality, you cannot compare the operation of this building with its conventional equivalent. They are totally different. You are not comparing apples with apples."

Within the client's brief to the design team there were two specific environmental targets. Firstly, the building had to achieve a BREEAM 'outstanding' rating, the highest possible. The Building Research Establishment Environmental Assessment Method is based on a point-scoring system that assesses not only the sustainability of the construction process but, more importantly, the ongoing operation of the building. The second target, a DEC 'A' rating, is concerned with energy efficiency. Using the same alphabetic colour-coded system that consumers see when buying their fridges and freezers, this rating would be displayed on a certificate at the entrance to the building.

For all those involved in making 1 Angel Square a reality, the achievement of BREEAM 'outstanding' and DEC 'A' ratings has been the result of numerous team meetings, a fair few robust discussions and the odd sleepless night.

Conventionally, the design team for a new office building might study the BREEAM checklist and decide which of the points were attainable within their budget. With 1 Angel Square, that process was turned on its head. The design team looked down the list and decided which points they had absolutely no chance of achieving before concentrating their efforts on the rest.

Mark Johnson, associate director at Buro Happold, mechanical and electrical engineering partners for the project, recalls: "Given the scale of the building, we were never going to get the BREEAM credits for use of daylight because the floor plates were just too large and light levels start to drop significantly within three or four metres of a window. Also, we were never going to meet the targets for use of recycled materials. There are some, but not enough, and you have to remember we are building a large-scale commercial development, not a small hut in the woods."

A unique fuel

Electricity was always going to be the key to meeting carbon emission targets. It was clear from the onset that a low carbon source of electricity, generated on site, was paramount.

"We knew that heating – and, indeed, cooling – were never going to be the biggest uses of energy," says Johnson, "as our building is better insulated than

"When the seed is crushed you're left with a yellow meal that has been used in the rations of dairy herds for many years. It's also used for margarine and some varieties of rape produce a particular type of oil which has medical and industrial properties.

Since rapeseed oil has been used as a biofuel it has had a massive effect on the demand for the crop and certainly in the last 10-12 years rape growing has become a lot more intensive. Indeed it's now as important – if not more so – as an income generating crop than wheat.

Agriculture is one of those primary industries where you can see the process all the way through from beginning to end. Preparing the seed, putting it in the seed drill, planting it, looking after the crop's health throughout the year, harvesting it and loading it onto lorries as it leaves the farm. And so now we have added another dimension because we know where it is going after it has left the farm. That's actually quite satisfying, and to know it is environmentally beneficial too."

Robin Nurse, Farm Manager
Stoughton Estate, Leicester.

most. Electricity to power the lights, the computers, the control rooms and the lifts was always going to be the biggest energy draw and so potentially the biggest contributor to emissions."

Electricity generated at power stations is incredibly inefficient. Before even entering the National Grid, one half of the energy generated is lost as heat and yet more is lost during transmission. By the time the power reaches the end user, there has been an immense carbon cost.

"To reach our BREEAM targets we had to have a CHP plant on site," says Johnson. Combined heat and power (CHP) is just that: an engine powered by fuel that would not only generate heat but also electricity. In this case, it was decided that a surplus would also be generated and sold back to the grid.

This income-generating potential of a carbon neutral power source helped to strengthen the business case for the extra upfront expense. But it was the choice of fuel to power the CHP plant that caused some headaches.

After gas was considered and quickly discounted – its carbon credentials were below expectations even before it was piped into the building – wood chip became the favoured fuel. As a biomass fuel, it would have ticked all the necessary boxes to achieve the BREEAM 'outstanding' rating, but to the dismay of the client and design team, the resulting DEC energy efficiency certificate would have displayed a mere lime green 'C' rating rather than the coveted dark green 'A'.

The solution was to specify a CHP engine that could burn a biofuel supplied by The Co-operative Group itself. As the Group owns its own farms across the UK, growing crops including wheat, soft fruits and potatoes, it was a short step to identify rapeseed oil as a home-grown fuel that would provide the power and heat for its own head office.

CHP plants are no longer unusual – the use of biofuels is well established – but the sourcing of fuel in this way is groundbreaking and sets 1 Angel Square apart. "I can't think of any other client that would have the facility to grow its own fuel on this scale," says Johnson. "It's a unique story."

"Because it's our farming business," says Co-operative Group energy boss, Nigel Holden, "we can influence every aspect of the fuel's production and transportation in incredible detail. We can insist on the use of one more carbon friendly fertiliser over another, for instance, and so achieve a much lower carbon footprint compared to a fuel from a third-party supplier."

Free heating and cooling

Even before the CHP plant is switched on, 1 Angel Square has been designed to take best advantage of whatever natural heating, cooling and lighting a typical Manchester day can offer.

It's a building with a double-skin façade – two sets of windows effectively. Between the inner and outer 'skins' is a maintenance walkway made from a horizontal metal grid. The walkway will be accessible to allow window cleaners to clean the insides of the expansive glass façades. But the horizontal grid also doubles up as a sun shield, a solar shading device that keeps direct sunlight off the desks and computers and prevents the building from heating up too much in the summer months. In winter, when the angle of the sun is lower and direct sunlight is more welcome, the walkways don't get in the way of the sunshine entering the building.

"The space between the two skins also acts like a duvet that we've put around the building," explains architect Mike Hitchmough. "We've included louvres at the top so we can control whether to keep the air in or let it out. During the winter, the louvres will stay closed so the trapped air is warmed by what sunshine there is, and in the summer we'll open the louvres so the warm air is expelled."

To test their calculations, engineers subjected a sealed prototype of the proposed double façade window panels to a propeller engine wind and 'rain' test.

Visitors to 1 Angel Square will be confronted by three large 'ship funnel' structures as they cross Angel Square and approach the front door. Masquerading as public art, these are the inlets to three 70-metre tunnels, or 'earth tubes', which take fresh air into the building's basement. Drawing air underground for any distance stablises its temperature, so on a summer's day, warm air will be naturally cooled, during the winter, cold air will be warmed by a few degrees. It's a simple, passive method to provide free heating and cooling and tick more BREEAM boxes.

From the earliest back-of-envelope sketches, Hitchmough always intended the head office's central atrium to act as a 'social glue' that would bind a previously disparate workforce together but also contribute to the building's environmental performance. "On a human level, it acts as a social connector, and on a technical level it works as one large duct, reducing the need for metres of pipework," he says. The original idea was for 'conditioned' air – it would already be cooled or heated depending on the season – to enter the atrium at the lowest level and percolate up and across the floor plates, eventually leaving at each level through adjustable louvres in the double-skin façade.

But Buro Happold's Mark Johnson recalls that the initial concept might not have been aesthetically pleasing. "When we looked at the number of grilles you would need at the bottom of the atrium it looked very cumbersome and not at all what the architects might have originally envisaged. I think they had a vision of a few small grilles tucked away somewhere, but the reality was very different. As engineers, we are notorious for spoiling architectural moments!"

The project team had a re-think and came up with a radical change just weeks before the foundations were dug. It was decided that fresh air to each floor should arrive through ductwork up each of the three central cores and then leave via vents in the atrium roof, with the atrium still being used to keep the fresh and stale air-streams apart from each other..

Cool water from hot

As well as producing electricity, the CHP plant is helping to both heat and, bizarrely, cool the building. Over the winter months hot water will be sent through ducts up each of the three cores, then under the raised floors to 'trench' heating grilles next to the windows – a similar scenario to domestic central heating. During the warmer months, however, the hot water is instead diverted to a piece of machinery known as an 'absorption chiller'. Best viewed as a large refrigerator, it uses a heat source to drive a chemical cooling process instead of being powered by electricity. Hot water in, cool water out.

Absorption cooling is not new. The principle was invented by a French scientist, Ferdinand Carré, in 1858 and was made commercially available in the 1920s. Albert Einstein even tinkered with the process in 1926 and designed an alternative known as the Einstein Refrigerator. For 1 Angel Square, the absorption chiller is ideal: heat from the CHP engine can be used all year round and, unlike conventional refrigeration, the chiller uses no electricity.

The first absorption chiller apparatus, invented in 1868, demonstrated how heat provides the energy source for cooling.

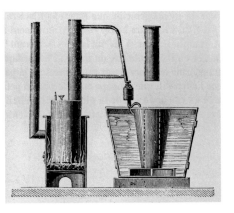

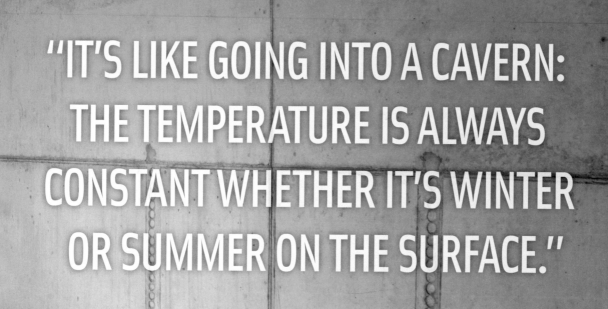

"IT'S LIKE GOING INTO A CAVERN: THE TEMPERATURE IS ALWAYS CONSTANT WHETHER IT'S WINTER OR SUMMER ON THE SURFACE."

Assembled off site, the 1,600 chilled beams were then positioned within the concrete 'coffers' in the ceiling. They provide both lighting and cooling and are controlled by sensors that detect whether the immediate vicinity is occupied.

The cool water is sent in two directions. It travels across the basement to cool the air arriving from the three earth tubes. On summer days, although the temperature of the incoming air will have been reduced a few degrees by its passage underground, it will still need additional cooling to maintain the target internal temperature of 20-21°C.

Cooled water from the chillers is also piped around the building to each of the 16,000 'chilled beams' which sit in the concave concrete coffers. Conventionally, a new building's mechanical and electrical services might be hidden from view. But increasingly, engineers are employing all-in-one chilled beams that deliver localised environmental control.

The 350,000 sq ft of concrete in the ceilings provides a passive cooling mechanism even before the chilled beams are switched on. Mike Hitchmough explains: "By getting as much thermal mass into the building – in this case, concrete – we are providing a sponge to absorb warm air. The warm air rises, hits the concrete ceiling and is absorbed into the ceiling. Once the ceiling has become saturated, only then do the cooling elements kick in. At night, as the temperature drops, the concrete slowly cools again ready for the next day."

Controlling the building

With all its low carbon, energy-saving innovations, will 1 Angel Square be too complicated a building to control efficiently? The project team are contractually committed to ensuring efficiency targets are met and maintained but it will be the occupier – The Co-operative Group itself – that will have day-to-day operational control.

Engineer Mark Johnson offers an analogy: "The project team has given the client the car and the engine, but if they drive it irresponsibly, they're not going to achieve the optimum fuel efficiency."

For The Co-operative, Richard Lewis, Building Services and Energy Manager with Initial FM, will be in the driving seat, with a pit crew of two electricians, two mechanical engineers and an apprentice. Between them, his team members have nearly 60 years of experience of the smooth running of Co-operative buildings in Manchester city centre.

"It's not a case of us being handed the keys on completion and being left to get on with it," says Lewis. "For many months we have been involved in the entire commissioning process, attending training sessions and workshops, so we have gained a gradual understanding and appreciation of all the building's intricacies. And neither is the project team walking away – their input will be vital in running the building effectively."

As staff are being relocated to the head office incrementally over several months, it will be some time before the efficiency of the fully occupied building can be properly assessed. And with different technologies coming into play throughout the seasons, assessments will vary from one month to another.

"It might be up to two years," says energy boss, Nigel Holden, "before we have it fine-tuned and working to its full potential."

"THESE WELDERS, YOU KNOW, ARE VERY EXPERIENCED. YOU CAN TIE THEM
TO A ROPE, DANGLE THEM UPSIDE DOWN OVER THE SIDE OF A BUILDING AND THEY
SHOULD STILL BE ABLE TO EXECUTE THE WELD. SO THE WELDING IS EASY,
IT'S THE INSTALLATION SEQUENCE THAT IS ALL IMPORTANT."

BETWEEN THE FOUR LARGE ROOF ARCHES ARE 54 PREFABRICATED 'LADDERS', THAT COME COMPLETE WITH CORROSION PROTECTION. 497 LOOSE 'RUNGS' ARE THEN WELDED LEFT AND RIGHT AND FORM THE LATTICE STRUCTURE. EVERY ONE OF THESE IS DIFFERENT.

Jan 2012

Tel: 020 7388 9777

CE08 YCP

"IN THE SUMMER THE OUTER SKIN IS THE FIRST LINE OF DEFENCE AGAINST SOLAR GAIN. IN THE WINTER IT BECOMES MORE LIKE A THERMAL BLANKET. SO IT WORKS HARD ALL YEAR ROUND."

"THE ROOF HAS 1,100 PANELS AND, AT OUR BUSIEST, WE WERE INSTALLING 300 IN A SINGLE WEEK. WE HAD THREE SPIDER CRANES AND OUR THREE TOWER CRANES ALL LIFTING GLASS PANELS AS FAST AS POSSIBLE SO WE COULD GET THE ATRIUM WATERTIGHT."

April 2012

"THERE'S NOTHING IN THERE THAT IS FUNDAMENTALLY NEW TECHNOLOGY. CONCEPTUALLY, WE'VE SEEN IT DONE BEFORE, BUT MAKING IT WORK FOR THIS BUILDING HAS REQUIRED QUITE A LOT OF INNOVATIVE THOUGHT."

"WE DELIBERATELY TILTED
IT TO FACE DUE SOUTH
TO GET WHAT SOLAR
GAIN WE CAN FROM A
MANCHESTER WINTER.
THE RAKED ELEVATION LETS
THE SUNSHINE IN AND GIVES
PEOPLE A FANTASTIC VIEW
SO THEY FEEL CONNECTED
TO THE CITY."

"THERE WERE CALLS FROM WORRIED PASSERS-BY TELLING US THAT OUR
WORKERS WERE STANDING ON THE EDGE OF THE BUILDING. WE REASSURED THEM
THAT THESE WERE SKILLED ABSEILERS AND – ALTHOUGH IT WAS HIGH-RISK WORK –
WERE NOT PUTTING THEMSELVES IN DANGER."

Leaving a Legacy

Not only would a £100m construction project have a significant impact on the regional economy at a time of recession, but the construction site itself could also become a focus for training, education and inspiration. The Co-operative Group understood this potential and, early in the process, identified opportunities with its partners.

Working with principal contractor BAM Construction, the Group set ambitious targets for both the number of apprentices the construction site would train and the number of contracts that could be awarded to local companies either directly or through a network of principal subcontractors.

From early in its appointment, BAM worked with Construction Industry Solutions to advise subcontractors on how best to identify and engage apprentices. A target was set for 8% of the total site workforce to be employed as apprentices. In addition, it was intended that 40% of the workforce would come from Greater Manchester.

BAM's Education Coordinator Penny Down says: "The construction period for the head office coincided with economic turbulence that was being felt most severely in the construction industry. Subcontractors who might have been reducing their skilled workforce because of the downturn were understandably reluctant to take on trainees. Despite that, we did well, taking on 32 apprentices – 7.6% of the workforce and just short of the ambitious target."

Down also points out that, on a project of such high technical complexity, the opportunity for entry-level workers is limited. Expert teams of specialists regularly travel the country, if not the world, to work for relatively short periods on one specific part of a complicated, high-tech contract. Despite this, the target for employment among local residents was exceeded, with 54% of the workforce coming from within Greater Manchester and 108 contracts awarded to local companies.

"There's a bigger picture on this site," Down continues. "As we have been able to help people into employment in different ways." BAM Construction responded to a call from Greater Manchester Police to support a project aimed at securing employment for ex-offenders. Two young men, not long released from prison, were identified as being ready for work and were employed on site. "One didn't work out," says Down. "The other, however, stayed several months, telling us that his time on site had been a life-changing experience and that without it, he might have reverted back to criminal activities."

Another young man was introduced to BAM through the Construction Youth Trust, a charity that helps young people find opportunities in the construction industry. Also an ex-offender, he was successfully engaged by a local roofing contractor.

As well as creating these paid employment opportunities, the site has accommodated work experience placements for young people at various levels, from secondary school students looking for experience of the workplace to unemployed graduates hoping to bolster their CVs.

Sean Seasman, an apprentice plumber with Rotary North West, was one of 32 apprentices to be employed on site.

"For any major construction company, engaging young people through educational activity has a long-term, knock-on benefit," says Down. "It's recognised that there is a skills gap in the industry, particularly on the professional and managerial side, and this is all about building up the workforce for the future."

Over the course of the construction process over 1,000 students were involved, engaged in more than 30 visits either to the site itself or by professionals to schools and colleges. "On all of these visits, the aim was very specific, whether it was a construction-related university course, a group of Year 10s who wanted to find out about careers in construction or a primary school group who wanted to understand a little more about the world of work," Down says.

Particular emphasis was placed on educational activities with the schools The Co-operative Group supports. "One technology college with a specialist interest in science and IT asked if someone would talk to students about how we use maths on a day-to-day basis," continues Down. "And so one of our engineers visited the school to do just that."

Other educational input has been more sustained. For The Co-operative Academy of Manchester – one of a handful of academies sponsored by The Co-operative Group – a couple of tailored workshops over the two-year construction period have had lasting results.

In 2011, students from the Academy were invited to contribute to a consultation on the design of the public space that would surround the new head office. Working with Scape, a consultancy that delivers educational workshops about architecture, students visited the site and, after being given an insight into the different roles on a construction site, considered the public space and who might use it.

"We visited and analysed other public spaces in the city centre and thought about how people might be attracted to a new space," explains Scape partner Charlotte Healey. "The students then came up with their own ideas, which they presented to a panel of architects and construction professionals. The panel was bowled over by some very sophisticated ideas."

Following this success a second workshop was commissioned in 2012. Interested students from different year groups came together to design a small structure for their school grounds. Fourteen-year-old Alessandra Ozuzu's design for a shelter-cum-outdoor classroom was selected and the wooden structure was built by BAM and its partners with the help of students on a basic construction skills course.

"The project opened the eyes of the students, some of whom had little or no experience of architecture or design," says Healey. "One young man, at first disruptive to mask a lack of confidence, went on to produce some of the most innovative ideas. A young woman, inspired by working on the shelter project, has since secured a placement at an architectural practice, where her contribution has been highly commended. Projects like these really do push the boundaries of young people's experiences and help realise their full potential."

During the construction period over 500 students visited the site including this group from the University of Manchester.

And what about schoolchildren who are not close to Manchester? How have they been engaged? The Group used the construction of its own head office as a starting point for a series of educational resources aimed at seven to 11-year-olds and linked to specific elements of the national curriculum. "Through the Green Schools Revolution, the Group already has a strong relationship with over 5,000 schools across the country," explains National Projects Officer Michelle Lockwood. "That programme supports registered schools by providing classroom and 'whole school' activities. The six 1 Angel Square modules include lessons around rainwater harvesting, solar energy, insulation and producing renewable energy with combined heat and power plants. My favourite is the 'past, present and future' module, which examines life in a Victorian school and compares that with today's education. Children are invited to imagine how education might change and even how an old school building might be refurbished using sustainable materials."

Throughout the building process, contractor BAM and The Co-operative Group supported Lifeshare, a local homelessness charity. With help from the project architects 3DReid and several of its sub-contractors, BAM refurbished the charity's city centre offices in a project worth over £15,000 in time and materials. "The old place looked like a police cell!" says Lifeshare's Judith Vickers. "But it's now been transformed from dark and old-fashioned to bright and modern, which has boosted the morale of both our staff and the young people we support." Following the renovation, much of which was carried out by apprentices from the head office site, The Co-operative Group contributed office furniture from its stores to complete the transformation.

The partnership has helped Lifeshare in other ways, too. The Group has made a substantial cash donation that has enabled the charity to help more than 60 young people into a bespoke educational programme that supports their subsequent progression into the workplace.

Staff from both the client and contractor have also got behind Lifeshare: Christmas gifts have been collected, money and food donations have been made and volunteers have helped serve meals to the homeless service users. Co-operative staff have passed on computer skills and even formed a working group to clean the Lifeshare premises.

Inspired by 1 Angel Square, students from The Co-operative Academy of Manchester designed an outdoor structure for their school and subsequently helped BAM and its partners build the chosen design.

A New Way of Working

On his appointment as Chief Executive in 2007, Peter Marks was determined that the renewed vibrancy of The Co-operative Group's core retail business – including the re-launch of the brand and the acquisition of Somerfield – should be reflected in an internal culture that matched the external dynamism. That culture, he acknowledged, could only be achieved if employees were accommodated appropriately and equipped with the latest technology.

As an existing board member, he was already familiar with the antiquated executive offices in New Century House but less so with many of the cramped, outdated office environments in which staff were struggling to meet the demands of the expanding business.

With over 3,000 staff across seven different buildings in the 'Co-op Quarter' of Manchester's city centre, the 'silo' mentality between departments was all too prevalent. Business teams were confined to inappropriate spaces that could not be adapted because of their listed status; meetings were held in windowless, airless rooms with obsolete equipment; and departments guarded by locked doors and entry phones did little to generate a sense of openness and transparency.

"1 Angel Square is designed to break down the silos and allow our colleagues to interact, move around and collaborate more effectively," says Amanda Jones, Head of Business Change and Transformation. "We'll better understand our colleagues and share ideas at a faster pace in our new building."

Indeed, the central atrium of 1 Angel Square – as well as playing a crucial role in air circulation – has been described as the 'social glue' that binds all the different head office departments together. Many floors and hundreds of colleagues – like worker bees in a hive – will be visible from any point overlooking the vast atrium.

Leading with technology

The short move across Miller Street marks a transformational change for the Group – a change in not only where Manchester employees will work but how they will work. The building's physical design and layout are integral to this change and the designers have put as much emphasis on facilitating efficient working practices as on meeting stringent environmental targets. Following extensive consultation, open plan offices, breakout areas, huddle spaces and quiet zones have all been included to give employees plenty of ways to work more productively.

But it is in the information technology (IT) systems that staff will see the most significant changes to their daily routines.

IT Project Manager Jim Phelan explains: "For many years, investment in 'back-end' IT infrastructure has not kept pace with the organisational demands of such a progressive business and so there has been an inability to support all the business groups effectively.

"For the new head office, we've introduced 'virtual desktop technology' which measn staff will no longer be attached to a particular desktop computer or laptop. They will be able to sit at any desk and log on at any desk and their applications, documents and email will all be available to them. They can work anywhere in the building and outside the building too: at home, in other offices and on the move, giving us a truly agile workforce."

The virtual desktop or 'thin client' technology, as it is known, consists of a keyboard, mouse and screen fitted with a small processing unit. The applications and data are stored in data centres off site, connected through temperature-regulated master control rooms in the basement. The desktop screen simply becomes a window into the server and, because little of the data processing takes place in the computers themselves, heat emissions are considerably reduced – another tick on the environmental checklist.

"We've made a huge investment in state-of-the-art technologies," Phelan says, "which will help all employees to work more efficiently." 'Follow me' telephony allows telephone calls to be automatically routed to the appropriate workstation, or diverted to a mobile or home number. Meeting rooms, too, will be fitted with the latest technology for AV presentations and conference calling. Staff will

Antiquated office accommodation did nothing to promote openess and transparency.

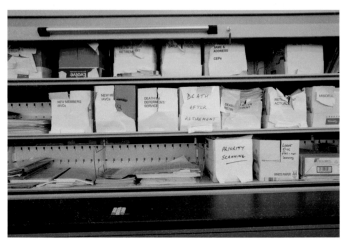

log on at the meeting room's terminal, access their personal desktop and, for instance, play their presentation directly to a TV monitor or screen. "The idea of carting around projectors, laptops and even pen drives will be a thing of the past," says Phelan.

Agile working is nothing new. Many large organisations have already embraced this working method. The idea that every employee needs their own desk is becoming a thing of the past. But for The Co-operative Group, cocooned for so long in outdated offices with obsolete technology, it's a major culture shift and a significant challenge – albeit one that has been comprehensively embraced. Rather than waiting for 1 Angel Square to be completed, Amanda Jones and her Business Change and Transformation team have progressively supported all departments to change their working practices. "When we move in, we will all be ready," she says. "It should be a case of walk in, log on and start working."

The change has not always been straightforward. Staff have needed to be convinced that they can do without their own desk or office, or team meeting room. Managers have had to be assured that their staff can be trusted to work in different ways.

"We all go through change without realising it," says Jones. "But when someone says, 'Would like you to change?' there is a natural resistance, a fear factor. However, we have already shown that this work style is more productive for our business and that people are enjoying the change. When they enjoy it and look forward to it, then it becomes sustainable."

As well as allowing the individual employee more flexibility and variety, agile working also provides huge financial benefits to the organisation. External meetings, holidays and illness all keep staff away from their base and internal surveys at the Group showed that desks were only ever occupied 50% of the time. Meeting rooms were used for no more than 15% of the day and less than half of all Manchester staff needed to be linked to a particular desk because of the nature of their work. Huge efficiencies could be made by servicing only those who were actually in the building at any one time. Why provide desk space, heating, light and computer systems to a half-empty building?

"After a series of consultations and surveys we came to the conclusion that our new building only needed 80 desks for every 100 employees," says Martyn Hulme, Managing Director of The Co-operative Estates. "By adopting agile working, we were effectively saving ourselves two whole floors of office accommodation."

More space will be saved by the implementation of a robust new strategy towards paper archiving. "We are on target to achieve an 80% reduction in the amount of paper we store," continues Hulme. "That is equivalent to 2,000 filing cabinets that we will no longer need."

As part of this new paper-handling process, all mail is now delivered to an external sorting office, where it is opened, scanned and emailed direct to the intended recipient.

Cramped and outdated: the existing office environment was deemed unfit for purpose.

"We wanted to ensure our real estate would work for us as efficiently as possible and so we developed new work settings that would 'de-focus' the desk and encourage colleagues to work in different ways.

"Three overall themes were originally considered – 'classic', 'modern' and 'sustainable' – and it was the sustainable palette that was approved and applied throughout the building."

One unified business

Although it is capable of accommodating 3,000 employees, 1 Angel Square was never intended to be the future home of all the Group's Manchester employees. The plan had always been for some departments to remain in existing accommodation that would be refurbished to modern office standards.

The new building would be predominately occupied by the food, pharmacy and funeralcare businesses, while also providing space for the corporate head office functions like marketing, finance and HR. The Group's financial services businesses would remain in their current buildings on Miller Street and Balloon Street.

NOMA Director David Pringle recalls: "We had a massive debate about whether or not we should build one or two buildings. A 328,000 sq ft building in the centre of Manchester is a huge piece of kit – most office buildings are a third of that size. Only a couple – the RBS building at Spinningfields and the Town Hall – come close.

"We briefly considered two separate buildings facing each other but that would have damaged the whole integrity of what we were trying to achieve from an occupational perspective. If we'd poured more people in, then it would've become too big."

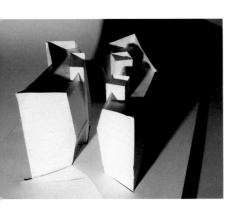

One building or two? With so many staff to accommodate, The Co-operative's team and its architects speculated on constructing two buildings facing each other and connected by bridges in a central atrium.

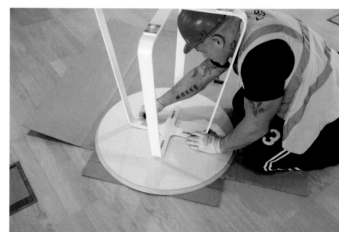

"THE PROCUREMENT OF THE CHAIRS IS A STORY IN ITSELF. WE NEEDED SOMETHING ERGONOMIC THAT WORKED WELL IN A FLEXIBLE ENVIRONMENT BUT DIDN'T HAVE TOO MANY LEVERS.

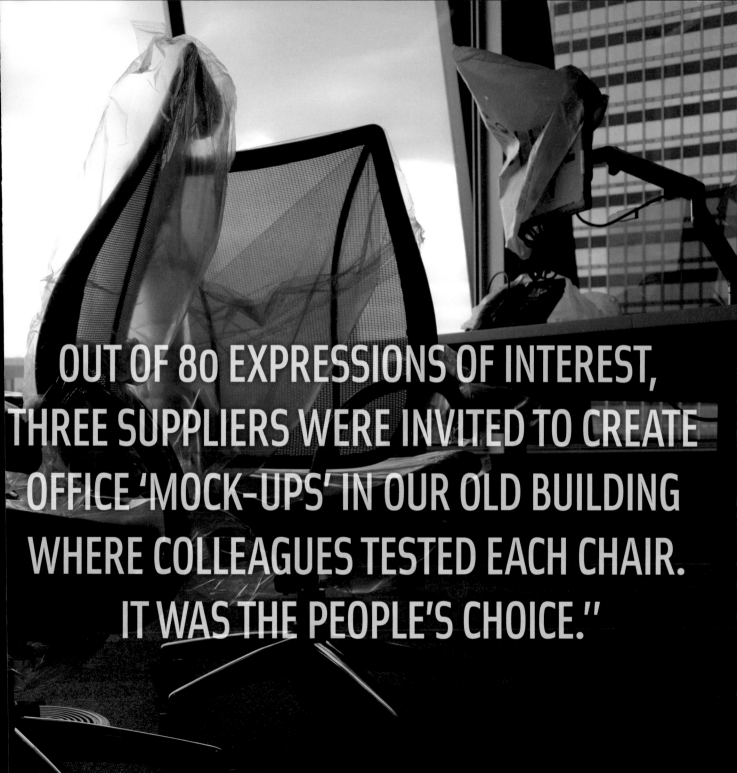

OUT OF 80 EXPRESSIONS OF INTEREST, THREE SUPPLIERS WERE INVITED TO CREATE OFFICE 'MOCK-UPS' IN OUR OLD BUILDING WHERE COLLEAGUES TESTED EACH CHAIR. IT WAS THE PEOPLE'S CHOICE."

Dec 2012

"THE BIGGEST CHALLENGE
WILL COME AFTER HANDOVER
WHEN THE BUILDING HAS
TO DELIVER THE HIGH LEVELS
OF SUSTAINABILITY THAT
THE BRIEF DEMANDS."

"WE DIDN'T WANT
A BUILDING SO
OVERBEARING IT
WOULD PUT PEOPLE
OFF COMING TO
JOIN US."

"THERE'LL BE A
LOT MORE
SHARING,
A LOT MORE
COLLABORATION.
IT'LL BE EASIER
FOR PEOPLE TO
COMMUNICATE
WITHIN THE
BUILDING."

"THERE HAS NEVER BEEN A BETTER TIME FOR US TO
BREAK THE LINK WITH THE INDIVIDUAL DESK."

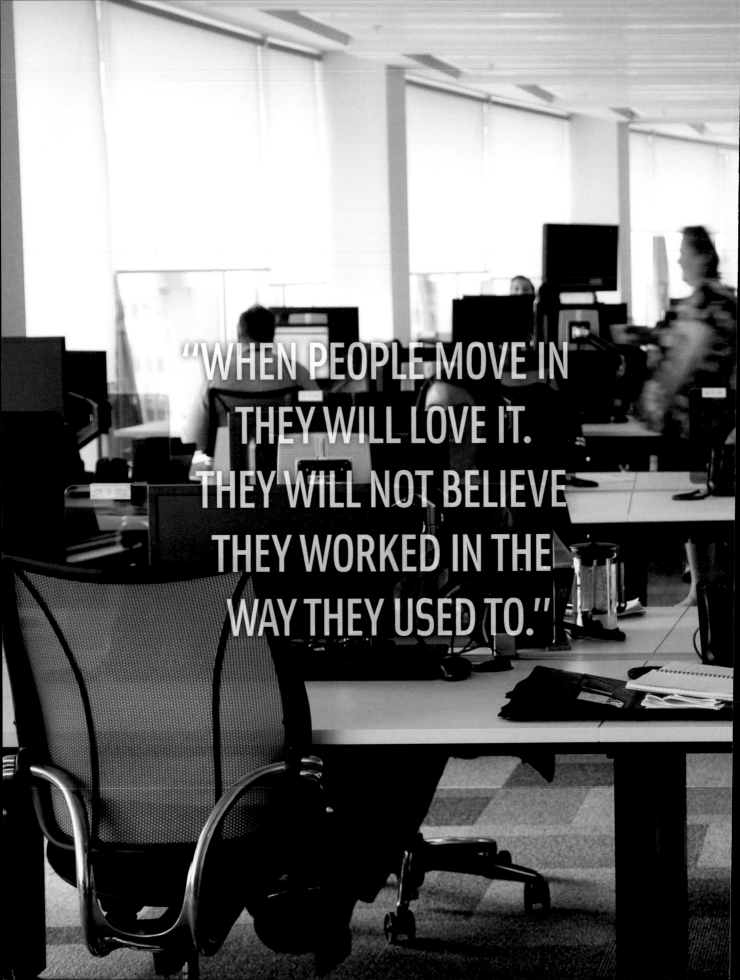

By 1904
membership of UK
consumer
co-operatives had
reached 2 million

1904

CWS employees formed a Thr
as a provision against old age

1905

CWS opened an Excursion
Department to assist socie
to arrange day trips and
holidays for members

"IT'S JUST THE BEGINNING, ISN'T IT? IT SETS A BENCHMARK FOR WHAT WILL COME NEXT."

1 Angel Square

Design Team:

Client:	The Co-operative Group
Principal contractor:	BAM Construction Ltd
Architect:	3DReid
Project management:	Gardiner & Theobald
Consultant engineers:	Buro Happold

Sub-contractors:

A Andrews & Sons	Wall and floor tiling
A E Yates	Hard landscaping
Airedale	Kitchen equipment and café fit-out
Alternative Access Logistics	Window cleaning cradles, fall protection
Ascot Doors	Metal doors
Ashlea Landscaping	Soft landscaping
Atwork	Feature wall
B&K Systems	Floor screeds
Charles Henshaw & Son	Curtain walling
Contract Blinds	Blinds
D Wilson Architectural	Architectural metalwork - spiral staircase
Delta Balustrades	Architectural metalwork - handrails and balustrades
DPL	Secondary steelwork
Firesafe	Fire protection
Fisher Engineering	Structural steelwork
Frontier Pitts	Automatic barriers
Fulcrum	Utilities
Gariff Construction	Specialist joinery
Gillespie	Auditorium ceiling
HT Scaffolding Systems	Scaffolding
Helix Industrial Roofing	Cladding
Helix Roofing Contractors	Roofing
Horbury Building Systems	Plastering, dry linings, ceilings
Hörmann Doors	Roller shutter doors
John Abbott Flooring	Carpet and vinyl floor finishes
Kingspan	Raised access flooring
Kone	Lifts
London Wall	Sliding folding partitions
McCrory Brickwork	Masonry

MGD Hygiene	Hygienic wall linings
Nationwide Joinery	Joinery, mirrors
Neslo Partitioning	Glazed partitions
P C Harrington	Concrete frame and pre-cast stairs and landings
PMJ Masonry	Stone cladding
Premier Asphalt	Road markings
Prospec	Lockers
RJ Edwards	Metalwork - ladders and fire escape stairs
Rotary North West	Mechanical and electrical services
Security Solutions	Turnstiles
Smiths Painters	Painting and decorating, specialist wall finishes
Solinear	Aluminium louvres
Sound Interiors	Glazed partitions and integral doors
Stonehouse	Specialist joinery
Swift Horsman	Toilet fit-out
Thorp Precast	Precast concrete - coffered slabs
Transco	Utilities
United Utilities	Utilities
Waagner Biro	Curtain walling, atrium roof, twin wall external façade

Building Awards

Builder and Engineer Awards 2011	Sustainable Project of the Year: Winner
Property Week Awards 2012	Sustainability Achievement Award: Winner
Insider Property Awards NW 2012	Sustainability Award: Winner
Green Apple Awards 2012	Built Environment, bronze level: Winner
Regeneration and Renewal Awards 2012	Sustainability Awards: Winner
British Council of Offices Awards 2012	Best Corporate Workplace (Northern): Winner
RAC Cooling Industry Awards 2012	Low Carbon Achievement of the Year: Finalist
Manchester Chamber of Commerce Property & Construction Awards 2012	Building of the Year: Finalist
BREEAM Awards 2013	Best Office: Winner
MIPIM Awards 2013	Best Office and Business Development: Finalist
RICS North West Awards 2013	Design & Innovation Award: Winner
RICS North West Awards 2013	Commercial Award: Winner
North West Insider Awards	Commercial Development of the Year: Winner
North West Regional Construction Awards 2013	Sustainability Award: Winner
North West Regional Construction Awards 2013	NW Project of the Year: Winner

Acknowledgements

Len Grant would like to thank all those who gave their time to be interviewed for this book. At The Co-operative Group: Peter Cookson, Nigel Holden, Martyn Hulme, Ruairidh Jackson, Amanda Jones, Moira Lees, Michelle Lockwood, Peter Marks, Kathryn Mitchell, Robin Nurse, Jim Phelan, David Pringle and Len Wardle. Also Jim Webster and Mike Hitchmough at 3DReid; Ian Fleming, Tony Grindrod, Dennis Whiteley and Penny Down at BAM Construction Ltd; Bernhard Reiser at Waagner Biro; Mark Johnson at Buro Happold; Bob Dyson at Jones Lang LaSalle; Richard Lewis at Rentokil Initial; Judith Vickers at Lifeshare; Julia Chance and Charlotte Healey at Scape; and Chris Wild at Oxford Archeology North. Many thanks to you all.

Thanks also to Gareth Brown, Robert Cohen, Andy Goodwin and Nicky Moore at The Co-operative Group; Rob Herold, Andy Robinson and Mike McCarthy at BAM Construction Ltd; David Maher at 3DReid; Deryck Jones, Fagan Jones Communications Ltd; Ian Miller at Oxford Archeology North; David Govier at The Manchester Room & County Record Office; and Alan Ward at Axis Graphic Design.

To all those who helped construct 1 Angel Square, thank you for your co-operation and good humour.

About the author

Len Grant is a Manchester-based freelance photographer and writer. He has documented the renaissance of the city for more than two decades and compiled numerous books and exhibitions about the construction of Manchester and Salford's most recent iconic landmarks.

With words and pictures he has charted much of the city's neighbourhood renewal programme, telling the stories of those affected by change. Most recently books and blogs about social exclusion have brought the lives of the least privileged to the fore.

www.lengrant.co.uk